How To Sew Art

Master The 9 Secrets For Transforming
Ordinary Fabric Into Fine Art & Profit

...the easy way!

Tammie Bowser

How To Sew Art

Master The 9 Secrets For Transforming Ordinary Fabric Into Fine Art & Profit

...the easy way!

by Tammie Bowser

Copyright © 2015 Tammie Bowser

Author: Tammie Bowser
Editor: Jan Emanuel, Denise Roberson, Angela Joyner
Book Design & Illustrations: Tammie Bowser

All quilts designed and made by Tammie Bowser except where indicated

Library of Congress Cataloging in Publication Data
Bowser, Tammie
      How To Sew Art / Tammie Bowser
      ISBN 978-1-887467-01-8 (paper trade)
      1. Quilting. 2. Quilting -- Art.
      3. Quilting--Applique.
      1. Title.
Library of Congress Control Number: 2014919771

Published by:
      Bowser Publications
      Post Office 1482
      South Pasadena, California 91031-1482

Printed in the U.S.A.

Hi Tammie,

Well, I finally finished my Rod Stewart wall hanging just in time for Rod's current tour. I was undecided whether to give it to him or not but I took it to the Vancouver concert to show it to him during the concert. The end result being that we went to his dressing room and I got to show it to him and he loved it. He said that we was going to get it framed, so needless to say I gave him the wall hanging and have a picture with him and the wall hanging. I also got a hug and 3 kissesfor my efforts.I really enjoyed doing the quilted photo and will have to do another one of Rod so that I can keep it. Everybody justs loves the results and are amazed that it is made of fabric.

Thanks again for showing me a wonderful way to reproduce my pictures using fabrics. Thanks

Jean Allbeury

P.S. Here is the photo with Rod, me and the wall hanging. Can you imagine something that I made will be framed and hanging in Rod Stewart's house.

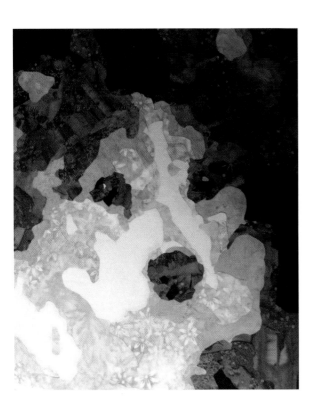

It was a fun class!
Hi Tammie, My name is Anne Gavin and I wanted to show you the piece I finished from your class at Hampton Roads in February. It was a fun class and I enjoyed it so much. Thanks for all your help.

Anne Gavin

We enjoyed your class very much. You made it so easy. We had so many great comments on the quilts we made. We are planning on making 6 more!
Martha Christensen & Cora Hall
Carson, CA

Dear Tammie,
I am thankful that your class was available. After ten years, it took my quilting to a higher level!
Ozellia Crawford
Los Angeles, CA

Quilted Photography is totally unique and exciting. It involves two things that makes me love quilting, it's looks hard but is really quite simple. And it is fun too!
Jan Emanuel
Pasadena, CA

I learned more about color value in the one day class than at Art School! Tammie's instructions were great! I watched my photo come to life in the class. I will treasure my quilt for a lifetime!
Darlen Lee
Acton, CA

I learned so much about the color value of fabrics! I now use this knowledge on other quilt blocks and wearable art. What a valuable addition to my quilting education! Thank You
Annette Berry
Los Angeles, CA

Tammie's method is ingenious! I was able to make a beautiful mosaic quilt in color from a black and white photo of my mother as a child from 1937. I created an heirloom quilt that will be in the family for generations to come. The technique is so simple even a novice quilter can create an incredible piece of textile art. I am currently working on another portrait, and plan to make quilts of more family members, this is addictive!
Thanks Tammie!
Cheryll Handy
Pasadena, CA

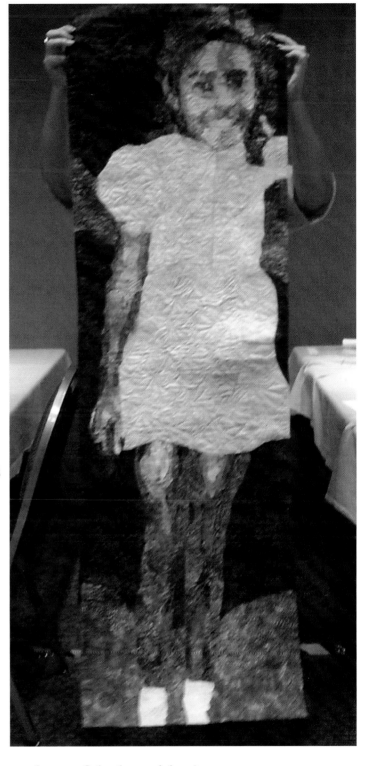

"Tammie Bowser's methods give you the tools to make heirloom-quality quilts on your first try. She has created a program that breaks down a process that would be unfathomably complicated for a busy quilter and makes it fun and fast to do. The results are nothing short of stunning in every case."
Sue Ann Taylor
Founder of Quilters News Network

"Your favorite photos recreated in fabric... what a fabulous idea! Tammie's easy to follow directions and her color value theories will help you preserve a memory in fabric"...
Kaye Wood
Television show host and author of 28 quilting books

Quilted Photography is just fabulous! Creating a quilt with your cherished photo on it is a great idea. My daughter Rosie (16 years old) and I have enjoyed making your quilts. It is something we enjoy doing together.
Kath Robi
Pasadena, CA

It was a fun experience to watch my photo "appear" as the fabric pieces were added!
Marcy Young
Sherman Oaks, CA

Tammie is a lovely, energetic & wildly creative woman! I thought quilted photography would be intense and difficult, but with amazing results only half of that is true, her technique is simple, clear and it does yield amazing results!
Alexis Durham
Manhattan Beach, CA

For a long time I had been trying to introduce pictures into my quilts, so I learned different techniques to make memory quilts. It was OK for a while, but your Quilted Photography was what I was looking for! It is a real picture experience. I LOVE IT!
Francisca Reynoso
Valley Glen, CA

I Loved your class. I did a combination of my 2 grandchildren. Everyone loves it. I had a lot of enjoyment working on it.
Jo Ann Felter
Buena Park, CA

These quilts are extremely easy and fun to make! They make great gift quilts. The instructions are easy to follow and your class was a lot of fun! This is a great quilt for any beginner or advanced quilter!
Sue Vite

I found the Mosaic Quilt Studio on the web and was simply floored by the images and possibilities. The class was fantastic and I continue to work on photo quilts. The quilt I made in class has won "First Place" in two shows, one "Judges Choice" and one "Best of Show"!
Marlene Pearson
Santa Barbara, CA

Thank you for inspiring me to make mosaic fabric photographs of everyone in my family for Christmas presents this year (2003). I began in January and by 11:30pm December 24th, I had finished eighteen! When I saw episode #819 of Simply Quilts, I called you on the phone and you were kind enough to spend quite a while encouraging me. Thanks again!
Peggy Johnson
Lake Oswego, OR

I certainly like the results of my taking your class. The ease of picking the colors and swatches to develop the picture was phenomenal! The class was well taught!
Sara Brandon
Los Angeles, CA

Making my mosaic quilt was fast, fun & easy. Not at all as hard as it looks. Everyone that sees my quilt is impressed, especially my six year old son (he is on the quilt). I can't believe I made it in one class. Can't wait to make my other two kids a picture quilt!
Debbie Hoshizaki
Los Angeles, CA

My quilt turned out beautifully - I didn't realize that my cat was ill when I started working on it. As I neared the end, he being quite ill, he sat with me as I finished the quilt. He died as I finished the quilt. I was able to have him near as our time together ended... The quilt sits above the piano now.
Ingrid Margolin
Glendale, CA

I've been quilting for 3 years and have never seen anything like your quilts, and I just had to take your class! It looked difficult but in fact is so easy and fun!! It was like paint by number but with fabric. Thanks for bringing this technique to us.
Debbie Sparr
Los Angeles, CA

"Tammie's quilted photos are so slick to make; they come together like magic! Besides being fun to make, It's fun to bask in all the compliments."
Ami Simms
Quilt book author, award winning quilter

Sherry Brady, Owings, MD

I had a great time making "Evan" my grandson. At first I thought this is not looking like anything and "pow" there he was. This work has won 2 awards. One for a quilt show and one for an art show. So exciting!

Thank you
Pat Carlson

PS Tammie your process is fun and exciting to do.

Tammie, Through you I have really found my artistic voice. I met you in Nashville and my art life has never been the same. This is an awesome technique! I LOVE IT!!!
Lisa Bova

Tammie, I really enjoyed making this quilt — it was such fun to see my husband come to life before my eyes! I made the quilt for a challenge project in our quilt guild. The theme was "When Quilters Talk, They Say It With Color." Blue is associated with depth and stability. It symbolizes trust, loyalty, wisdom, confidence, intelligence, understanding, integrity, seriousness, and truth — all attributes that describe my husband. The technique used to make the quilt also represents Al's ability to move beyond the minute details in order to see the big picture of any situation. He is my true blue love, so I named the quilt, My True Blue You/Love Is Blue. Thanks for providing a terrific computer program that helped make this quilt so much fun to make!
Annie Unrein

Tammie, I wanted to share my first quilt with you. I have been thinking about making a quilt for several years, but didn't feel I had the time. When I saw you on Sewing with Nancy, I immediately looked for your website as I knew that this process would be relatively quick. I loved pressing the pieces on and seeing the pattern come to life. Thanks for your software and your quilting process. I have attached both my quilt and the photo I used for the pattern.
Regards,
Shari Sands

"These quilts are extremely easy and fun to make! They make great gift quilts. The instructions are easy to follow and your class was a lot of fun! This is a great quilt for any beginner or advanced quilter!"
Sue Vite

Table Of Contents

Dedication

Thank you to all of my past students for sharing your photos and comments.

I want to thank God for the endless source of creative ideas.

Finally, I want to dedicate this book to my Grandaddy, Wally Taylor.

When I was a vendor for the very first time at International Quilt festival in Houston, I was really afraid to go alone. I didn't know if I would be accepted with my unusual ideas, so I asked my Grandaddy to go with me and he did! I think he talked to every one of the 50,000 people who attended the show that week. He invited all of them to come in my booth to see my stitched art!

Granddaddy,
Thank you so much for loving and always encouraging me. I love you and I miss you.
Thank you for being my Grandaddy.

July 1929 to October 2012

Becoming An Artist

I started sewing when I was 4 years old. I remember my pre-school teacher Mrs.Smith asking me what I wanted to be when I grew up. My answer came without thinking. My response was automatic. I told her that I was going to be an artist. I just knew it.

I don't remember deciding to sew but I do remember my grandmother teaching me how to make a running stitch with a needle and thread. I got so much joy from sewing my purple velvet mini skirt and matching vest.

I lived with my family in the projects of South Central Los Angeles. Creativity became my way of escaping the realities of my young life.

The days were so long then. I remember spending whole days trying hard to breath. There were so many days when the asthma would make my throat feel like a thin straw that only allowed in tiny bits of air. My mom told me that sometimes my hands and feet would turn blue. I would close my eyes and reach deep into my heart and ask for help. Then sometimes I would just pop right out of my body!

I Was Holding Hands With Angels

When I opened my eyes, she would be right there holding my hand. The angle came often. Sometimes I could see my sick body lying in a bed across the room. Sometimes I would fly above my school watching the kids on the playground. I could breath again for a little while and we would sing songs together or play together when I was to sick to go outside to play. It felt really good to step away from the heaviness of my body. I could feel love. I could see angels. I could hear God.

I'm blessed to still remember.

Late one night, when I was about 7, I was awakened by the sound of my fathers angry voice. My mother was arguing. I got out of my bed, walked past my little sister and brother towards the living room. I saw their big shadows. Then I heard him hit her. I could feel my heart breaking.

I don't even know how to describe the sound of my mothers cry. I crawled under my bed, as far back into the corner as I could get. I called out to my angel for help and fell asleep holding her hand.

I Was Afraid

I began to notice my Mom crying more and more. I became aware of the danger we lived with. The danger that surrounded us because of my father, the alcohol and the heroin. Sometimes the fear would trigger the asthma and I would start wheezing and struggeling to breath again.

It seemed as though the fear became louder and louder. Like I could hear it ringing in my ears. At the same time, it became harder and harder to hear the voice of my angels. I stuggled to remember the songs we sang together. I tried hard to remember their faces.

I Had To Be Brave

Early one morning, my mom woke up us kids and told us to pick out three toys each. She packed our clothes, all that she could fit in the trunk of her car and drove away... away from the danger.

We also left our house, furniture, friends, all family and our identities. We moved to a place where we didn't know anybody. I missed my family. I missed my daddy.

I tried to be a good girl so that my mom would stop crying. I was just 7 but I had to help with my little sister and brother. I had to be brave.

Sometimes I would ask my angels for help but I couldn't see them any more. I missed them.

Even though we were really poor, I always had a needle and thread. I still made things. I began to cut up old clothes to make dolls, or anything I could think of. Sewing gave me relief from the requirement to be grown up and mature. Sewing let me reach into my imagination and pull out something good. I could escape from my sadness. It felt good. It felt like I had found an old friend.

Creavity Was My Friend

I remember the last time I got sick... my last asthma attack. I was 12 and in bed for a full month. Then I learned how to use a sewing machine. I'm not sure if the sewing machine made me better or not but it sure seemed like it!

When I was in high school I would go to the Salvation Army to buy designer jeans for cheap. I'd then tear them apart and make them fit me perfectly! It was so easy...

When I had a bad day, I learned to always reach into my heart, the place where I keep my creativity and pull out a wonderful idea. My ideas were my treasures. I started to trust my ideas because It felt good. I even started to see my angels again... in my dreams. I couldn't see their faces but I recognized them by how they made me feel.

I Had To Find Courage

As high school was ending, my mom told me that she and her husband were selling the house and moving 200 miles away. I needed a plan because I needed a way to take care of myself. I chose to follow my heart and my talent...
I went to fashion school.

Since I was now on my own, I decided to change my name back to Bowser. I needed

to get my identity back. I missed my family
all of the years that I was away from them. So I went to find them and my
father.

I Thought I Had Life All Figured Out

I was studying fashion design and living on my own at 18 years old. I
thought that my life would be perfect if I could find my dad. In my mind, I
amagined that he was all clean and strong... like Superman!

My long lost cousin asked me if I wanted to see him and I answer "Yes, I
have to see him". She took me to a house and I knocked on the door. I heard
a male voice saying "Who Is It?" I said "I'm looking for Melvin".
Time slowed down as I waited for him to come out of the strange dark
house. I had not seen my daddy's face for over eleven years. When he came
out he wasn't Superman, he wasn't better, my heart was broken.

I Was Lost

It took me a while to recover. I went back to my creative studies. I
developed a career in fashion, traveled the world and bought myself a
house.

Years later, I got married. I found myself with a small baby and divorcing.
I'd always told myself that I'd do things the right way. I had failed.

After spending a year at home with my baby, I needed to make money
again. I tried to go back to the comfort of my creativity. I tried to find a job
in the career that had taken care of me for over 16 years but no one called
me back.

I had to do something, but had no idea how to make things better. I decided
to go for a walk. I put my baby in the stroller and I started walking and
talking to God. I reached down deep into my heart the same way I'd done
when I was small. I said "Please help me! Give me an idea, tell me what to
do".

I was hoping for a new job to appear... or maybe the bills would just vanish but that's not what happened. A few days later, I woke up with an idea!

The Idea That Changed Everything!

I don't remember dreaming. In fact, when I opened my eyes I was already sitting up in my bed. At that moment, I knew how to sew art.

The idea... the blessing, hit me like lightning!... but the mortgage was due and I still had no job. Then the next day, I got a call from an old work friend. I had not heard from Elizabeth in years! She said she found my old resume and wanted me to come talk to her. So I did.

Elizabeth gave me a $62,000 a year part-time job! Elizabeth was an angel delivering a gift from God that day. The feeling was unbelievable. God had responded to me. He heard my call for help.

I Had Everything I Needed

From the beginning, I'd only ever made clothes. I never even thought of sewing as art before. Now sewing art was all I could think about! I could feel my fashion career becoming less important. I was finally becoming an artist.

When I thought about the new idea, I knew that it was also my job to share it with other people. I had to share it with as many people as possible so I decided to write an email to Alex Anderson. She was the host of the popular television quilting show "Simply Quilts". A few months went by, then I got an email from a producer. She had invited me to be a guest on T.V.!

Sharing The Blessing

Before I taped my episode of "Simply Quilts", I knew that I needed to have a book. I didn't have enough time to write a book before my scheduled time on the set. So I made a book cover and taped it over the cover of another book!

I knew I could publish the book myself and that is what I did.

I started teaching people the new idea. I taught them how to make stitched art and I used my book as the textbook! The book sold really well and eventually became an Amazom 1# best-seller.

At first I thought my adventure into quilting would only last a short time. But the short adventure grew into my new career as an artist.

It seems like the more I share the ideas... the more ideas I get!

Now when I need help the angels don't hold my hand like when I was a little girl. They help me in a different way. They deliver ideas as I am sleeping. Then I wake up to find more amazing creative treasures.

I Am An Artist!

Along the way, as I kept following the flow of creative treasures, my stitched art was purchased by the Shelbourn musuem in Vermont and I was also chosen as the winner of the Japan award for Quilt National '07

This book you're reading is my 5th book. The chapters are full of the treasures delivered by my angels.... and the results are magical!

You Can Become An Artist Too.

The first thing you can do to become an artist is ask for ideas. Ideas fall down from heaven like rain drops. Start looking for them and act upon them because they will evaporate if you don't. You MUST treat the ideas that fall upon you like treasures because that is what they are. If you ignore them, you won't notice that YOUR CREATIVE BLESSINGS are sitting right in your lap!

On my journey so far, Art has been my friend, it has comforted me, it has taken care of me, it has been everything. Art is how God speaks to me... Art is LOVE

The journey is not over... stay tuned, more ideas are on the way and it's pleasure to share them with you !

A Note To The Reader

My intention is to make learning the lessons in the book a magical experience. I want you to feel like you've just enrolled in a workshop that will transform you into an artist! Follow the textbook (this book) and study the video lessons and you will have amazing success... I Promise!

What you are going to learn is the technique I used to win the Japan award at Quilt National '07. Two of my quilts were also pictured in the book "500 Art Quilts: An Inspiring Collection of Contemporary Work". My quilts were selected by Karey Bresenhan from Quilts, Inc. Karey is one of the most prominent figures in quilting.

Please read the book completely, and in sequence before starting your own projects. All of the core concepts and success secrets are critical for your success.

If you have any comments or questions that are not answered in the following instructions, please go to my support website to ask me personally: **www.TammieBowser.com**

How To Use Fabric Like It's Paint

In this chapter
- Color vs. Value
- Using Color For Impact
- Color Value Is The Key To Success!

I have respect for the work of the old master painters like Vincent Van Gogh. I get ideas from the surreal artist Salvador Dali. I am also inspired by contemporary artists like Andy Warhol, Chuck Close and especially Gustav Klimt. Gustav Klimt's work has many patterns, textures and colors. His work inspired me for the technique I will teach you in this book. I suggest that you look up each of these artists on the internet to see examples of their work. The more art you see, the more you will be influenced. Without any conscious effort, aspects of their work inspire me to try new things. I've been influenced by all of them.

Now I will teach you how I use fabric just like it is paint! It is possible and it is also easy if you take time to understand the core concepts in this chapter.

Color vs. Value
You know what color is (we will talk more about color in a moment) but do you know what color value is?

Core Concept #1 - Color value is

how light or dark a fabric is in relation to the other fabrics around it. To make art with your fabric you will have to create a color palette. You will use color value to choose you color palette. A color palette is the collection of fabrics used to make your stitched art.

When you choose the fabrics for you palette of fabrics, the most important step is arranging your collection of fabrics in order from the lightest to the darkest.

Core Concept #2 - For this technique to work you will always sort your fabrics from light to dark, because every image is like a black and white picture containing fabrics to represent black, white and all of of the shades of gray in between. (note: the fabrics represent black, white and gray. I always use light, medium and dark colored fabrics.)

I have found that it is hard for some students to determine the color value of fabrics. They are easily fooled by all of the colors. To solve this problem, I have designed three techniques that will allow you to see the values of your fabrics with ease.

#1 - Photocopy Technique
Cut a small piece of the fabrics you will be using. Use the Photocopy forms that you can download at: **HowToSewArt.com/bonus**

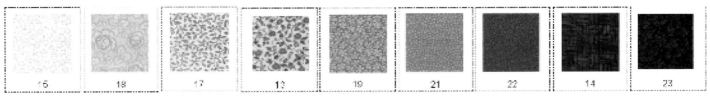

You can also find the forms at the end of this chapter. Print the forms, then tape one fabric piece in each of the boxes. Make a black and white photocopy of the forms.

IMPORTANT: The copy machine must capture grayscale. The photocopy will erase the colors, and only show you the value. Cut the photocopied swatches apart, and arrange them in order from light to dark. Now it will be very easy to see the correct order of the swatches. If two of your swatches look like they have the same color value, then make your decision about which fabric is lighter and which is darker by looking at the colors. You will use the numbers on the forms to identify the fabric order. Apply a sticker to each fabric and number them with number one as the lightest up to the darkest.

The value isolation technique works because you isolate the fabrics and only focus on two fabrics at a time. I have prepared a video demonstration for you. Watch the video to see the Value Isolation Technique in action. You can also get a Valuation Isolation Postcard for FREE Look at the back of the book for more details.

#3 - Use Your Computer!
I have also designed a software program to sort your fabric for you! All you'll have to do is import your fabrics and click a button! Watch this video to see a demonstration. **HowToSewArt.com/bonus**

Student Special Deal: If you complete a short quilting survey , I will give you a huge 50% discount on this simple to use Color Value software. Here's the student special link: **HowToSewArt.com/valuesurvey**

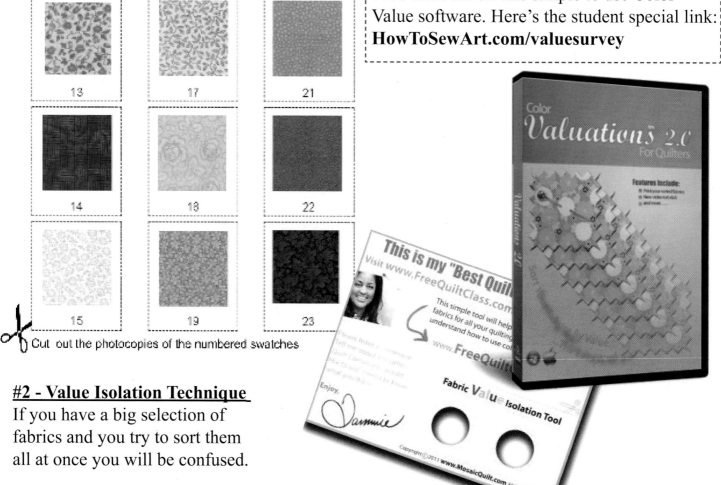

Cut out the photocopies of the numbered swatches

#2 - Value Isolation Technique
If you have a big selection of fabrics and you try to sort them all at once you will be confused.

Once you have your fabrics in order by color value, your success is guaranteed! Not only is color value very important but it is even more important than the colors you choose!

When you follow any of the three techniques to sort your fabrics, you will effortlessly create highlights, shadows, and depth in your stitched art.

Now lets talk about color and how you can use it to create art! This is my observation... You can easily mimic a picture or photo out of fabric... but using exact colors and copying them as you see them is not art. It is just a copy.

Core Concept #3 - When you choose your palette of fabrics, you can automatically transform your image into art by manipulating the colors.

Using Color For Impact

When you are planning a new project, you also need to focus on the colors because people are influenced by them before anything else.

You may have never thought of this subject before but different hues can influence your physical and mental states. Colors also influence the emotion you feel when you look at art.

Core Concept #4 - Using color to choose the kind of impact you want to make is easy and one of the most important factors you need to consider when deciding on your fabric palette.Here is a list of colors and what they mean:

Brown Tones earthy tones such as brown convey comfort, simplicity, and credibility.

Blue represents longevity and security. Researches show that blue brings a calming effect and suppresses appetite. Men usually love blue.

Vibrant Red represents high energy and vitality. Red also commands attention. It is exciting and passionate. Women are inclined to like red. Warning: Red is strong and can dominate a color palette.

Orange is friendly and playful. It is casual and full of energy. This hue will certainly demand the viewer's attention.

Yellow is welcoming. It will surely uplift one's energy. It feels warm and cheerful. It is very effective and beautiful when placed beside a dark background.

Green is representative of comfort, health, and growth. It is calming and restful to the eyes.

Black is a powerful and formal color and it can show high style.

Grey is safe. It is reliable, mature, and somewhat predictable. Grey is also used to give a modern look to your image.

White is simple, clean, attractive, and precise.

Color Value Is The Key To Success

Core Concept #5 - When you look at art, you instantly notice color. This can lead you to think that color is the most important thing to consider, but color value is the tool that will allow you to create perfect images. If you use value correctly, wise color choices will add impact and excitement!

Photocopy/Color Value Swatch Form

IMPORTANT NOTES: Copy must be grayscale so that you can see the values in varying shades of gray. First photocopy these forms, then attach your fabric swatches to the squares with tape or glue. Cut out the photocopied swatches. Arrange them in order by color value.

Attach Fabric
Swatch Here

1

Attach Fabric
Swatch Here

2

Attach Fabric
Swatch Here

3

Attach Fabric
Swatch Here

4

Attach Fabric
Swatch Here

5

Attach Fabric
Swatch Here

6

Attach Fabric
Swatch Here

7

Attach Fabric
Swatch Here

8

Attach Fabric
Swatch Here

9

Attach Fabric
Swatch Here

10

Attach Fabric
Swatch Here

11

Attach Fabric
Swatch Here

12

How To Sew Art Quiz #1

What Are The 5 Core Concepts We Discussed In This Chapter?

Core Concept #1 _____

_____

Core Concept #2 _____

_____

Core Concept #3 _____

_____

Core Concept #4 _____

_____

Core Concept #5 _____

_____

What Are The Three Ways To Sort Fabrics By Color Value?

Technique #1 _____

Technique #2 _____

Technique #3 _____

To see the color value video, go to: HowToSewArt.com/bonus

Pixels Are Magic!

In this chapter
- What Is A Pixel?
- What Are Magical Contoured Pixels™?

Read this chapter carefully because really understanding how to use pixels can be the difference between creating an average quilt or a stunning and magical masterpiece!

What Is A Pixel?

While studying graphic design, and computers I discovered that computerized photographs are not really photographs at all. They are just small squares of color that are arranged in a way that causes you to see an image. When I looked up the definition online, here is what I found: **A pixel is a physical point in an image, or the smallest addressable element of a picture.**

This concept works if you are using fabric, tile or even bottle caps! It also works if the pixels of color are dots, stars, triangles or any other shape... the shapes do not really matter. If you want to test this theory, just find any book, newspaper or magazine, and examine a photograph with a magnifying glass. You will see small dots.

To explain it further, the more squares that are used to create the image, the clearer the image appears. This is called resolution.

Even though we can see millions of colors, and most of the printed photographs you see in books and magazines have many thousands of pixels in them, it would be a nightmare to manage a project that has hundreds of different fabrics and millions of pixels!

I have experimented with different numbers

of fabrics. The number of fabrics that I have found to be manageable for the technique in this book is 12 or less. This number of fabrics will make your Stitched Art projects beautiful, and intriguing!

<u>**Core Concept #6**</u> - Use 12 fabrics or less and your art project will be easy to make!

What Are Magical Contoured Pixels?

You are probably wondering what is a "Magical Contoured Pixel™"? Well, when you look at a digital image in a normal way, you will not notice the pixels. That is because your eyes automatically blend the pixels together.

<u>**Core Concept #7**</u> - To make "Magical Contoured Pixels" we always blend the pixels together in an artistic way!

We've already learned that your project becomes more like art when you manipulate the colors. Well another important way to make your project more artistic is to manipulate the pixels by blending them together. When we blend the pixels together the magic begins to happen!

Here are some examples... We will start with a photo of the Mona Lisa.

Here is the same picture pixelated. It looks very digital... not very pretty. It has several thousand little squares.

Pixelated Picture

On the next page is the same image again with the pixels merged together with only 9 values/colors! The change is dramatic! It has only 300 pieces of fabric and it can be simplified to have even fewer pieces.

Picture with Magical Contoured Pixels™

How To Sew Art Quiz #2

What Are The 2 Core Concepts We Discussed In This Chapter?

Core Concept #6 _____

_____

Core Concept #7 _____

_____

Success Secret #1 - Pick A Good Subject

In this chapter

- Choosing An Image
- Taking Better Photographs
- Nature & Other Objects
- Flowers
- Portraits
- Free Contoured Pattern
- How To Make Contoured Pixel Patterns

In the first two chapters you learned 7 of the big core concepts. These core concepts help you understand why this technique works! You'll learn two more core concepts in chapter 6.

Now I want to begin teaching you the Success Secrets! The Success Secrets will give you the skills to successfully use the core concepts.

Choosing a great image is the first **Success Secret** and it is important because choosing the right kind of photo will make your success automatic.

Choosing A Image

The first rule that must be considered while choosing a photo is the light balance. It is ideal to have a balanced photograph that is not too light or too dark. If the light areas of the image are really light, or if the dark areas are excessively dark, you will not be able to see the details of the image. If the image has a minor imbalance, it can be adjusted, but if the image is far out of balance, your quilt will not have clear details.

Now lets consider the subject of your art quilt. The best images have one focus. If you have many things in the image, your

Balanced Photograph

Light Photograph

Dark Photograph

finished art piece will not have much impact because you won't know where to look. For example, take a look at the photo of the Grand Canyon on page 36 ... where do you look? Now look at the kitty picture above. You know right where to look! There are no distraction and it has immediate impact.

Here are some more ideas for good subjects for your Stitched Art.

Faces and hands happen to be my favorite images to quilt. They can be done with any color palette or even a color combination that will match the colors of a room. The more outrageous the color, the more artistic people will think you are!

Chapter 3

Animals or animal faces are also fun to do. Animals with fuzzy fur are best portrayed in color combinations that are realistic. If you use a random color palette for an animal, the image may be hard to see. If the animal has smooth fur or skin, any color combination that you choose will work fine. These are just my opinions. I urge you to be creative in your fabric and color choices because this is the most creative part of the process.

Landscapes and Buildings have a lot of small details, so they need to have lots of dots (higher resolution) to create the image. This also means that they will be larger because they have many more pixels. Images of buildings can have any colors you choose, but the landscapes should have a realistic palette.

Nature like a tree or even a flower, are best portrayed with a single color or realistic colors.

Other Objects like a musical instrument can be portrayed with any colors.

I really love old family pictures, but you can easily take new snap shots. You might want to consider using a digital camera or smart phone to capture images for your stitched art. The photographs will be created instantly and you can keep taking pictures until you get images you like.

It is also possible to find great photos on the internet for FREE! Getting permission to use the photos is important because it is illegal to steal photos without permission. Go to your search engine and look for "photos, creative commons."

You will find a lot of sites but my favorite is **Flickr.com.** Be sure to put the search setting to "creative commons" so that you'll have permission.

Another place to look for photos is Google Images. Go to **https://images.google.com** and search for any kind of image you might want. Click the "Options" button in the upper right corner. Then select "Advanced search". Next, scroll down the page and click the "Usage Rights" drop down box. Select the approiate permission level.

Taking Better Photographs
Although I am not a photography expert, I do know what kind of photographs work best for Quilted Photography.

Digital cameras are so simple to use, and the processing time is cut down to almost zero. It is possible to make great photos for stitching, as long as you have the right instruction. After reading this section, you will be able to spot a good photo or a bad photo for stitched art.

32   How To Sew Art

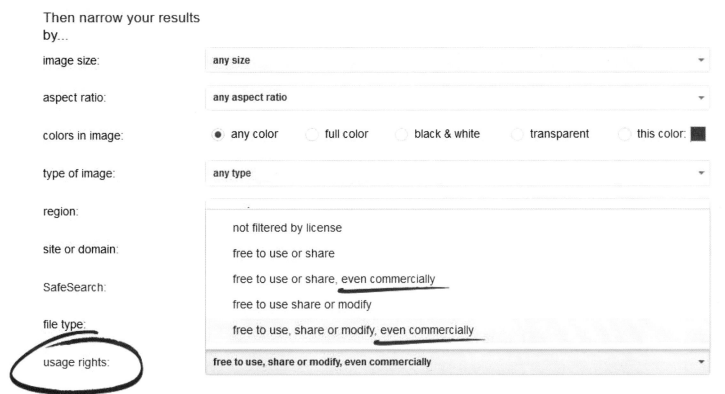

Then narrow your results by...

image size: any size

aspect ratio: any aspect ratio

colors in image: ● any color   ○ full color   ○ black & white   ○ transparent   ○ this color: ■

type of image: any type

region:

    not filtered by license

site or domain:

    free to use or share

SafeSearch:

    free to use or share, even commercially

    free to use share or modify

file type:

    free to use, share or modify, even commercially

usage rights: **free to use, share or modify, even commercially**

A great photo to use will have one light source. The light should come from one side, not from a flash on the top of the camera. A flash on the camera will shine a strong light right on the front of the face of a person, washing away all of the shadows, details, and contours.

A better way to create the right kind of light is to sit by a window. The light will shine in from one direction and you can see the results before you even take the photo. If the shadow is not dark enough, get a dark cardboard or piece of fabric and hold it on the side of the subject that the shadow should be. The darkness of the cardboard will absorb the extra light.

Another way to get great light is to go outside and use the early morning or the late afternoon sun. A good rule to follow is take your photos before 10am or after 2pm.

The mid-day sun will wash away all of the shadows, details and contours.

For each of these lighting tips, pay attention to how the light is shining on your subject, and move around until you like how the light is shining on your subject.

Remember that shadows and light are equally important. When you include both shadow and light in your photos the quilts will be well balanced and pleasing.

This baby photograph is a good example of the light source coming from one side, and it also has interesting shadows. The light is coming from the left and the shadow is on the right.

Portraits

When choosing a picture for a portrait, look for a person doing something they love! This man and his guitar is a good photo for this technique because the lights and shadows are interesting and he looks happy. Photo by Tom Marcello

The picture below would also make a great subject because of the interesting light and the beautiful wrinkles and beard. Photo by Örlygur Hnefill on Flickr.com

The **Contoured Pixel**™ technique makes it possible to make portraits with two faces like this one! This is a beautiful photo because the girls are displaying so much happiness. It really is amazing that the emotion on their faces is translated in fabric! To see this finished quilted art portrait, look in the **"Gallery Of Contoured Pixel**™ **Art"** on page 84. If you want to see the stitching close up, go to the website at: **HowToSewArt.com**

Nature & Other Objects

When choosing a picture of something in nature you still need to look for a single focused item. I love this tree because of the beautiful trunk and roots. This photo also has great light and shadows. Photo by Dave Eadie

To see this finished quilt, look in the **"Gallery Of Contoured Pixel™ Art"** on page 87. If you want to see the stitching close up, go to the website at: **www.HowToSewArt.com**

If you choose a large landscape like this one of the Grand Canyon, it will need to be very large to capture any details... and there is no focus. I would not recommend a photo like this one for the techniques in this book. Photo by W. Tyson Joye

You can also make stitched art of objects like musical instruments or cars or even a building. This trumpet is a good example because it has interesting reflections that translate well into to stitched art.

You can easily find pictures like this to use when you search for "creative commons" online. I found this trumpet photo this way.

To see this finished quilt, look in the **"Gallery Of Contoured Pixel™ Art"** on page 86. If you want to see the stitching close up, go to the website at: **HowToSewArt.com**

Flowers
I love flowers, but choosing a good photo can be tricky because they have many small details. The way I make the pictures work is by focusing on one flower and cropping the background.
Photo by Brian Fagan

To see this finished quilt, look in the **"Gallery Of Contoured Pixel™ Art"** on page 81. If you want to see the stitching close up, go to the website at: **HowToSewArt.com**

Free Contoured Pattern
This flower became stunning stitched art and only has 6 fabrics. After purchasing this book you can download the pattern when you register for the online video class at **HowToSewArt.com**

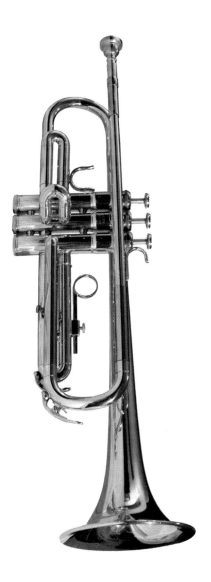

How To Make Magical Contoured Pixel Patterns

You can easily make your own Contoured Pixel™ Patterns with my Quilted Photography™ Software. You can download a fully working trial version of "Quilted Photo Deluxe" for FREE at: **HowToSewArt.com**

This FREE trial is really great becasue you can make as many patterns as you want for 7-days! Compatible with Mac and PC.

When you sign up for the FREE trial, you will also get an online video course!
The amazing video course is taught by me and I will deliver it directly to your email.

Continue reading to see how to use the software to make Magical Contoured Pixel™ patterns from your own photos.

Step by Step Instructions

Step #1 - Click "New Project" to clear the screen.

Step #2 - Import your photo.

Step #3 - Select the number of fabrics you want to use. (remember to use 12 or less!)

Step #4 - Select the pixel shape. Note: You can select any pixel shape you want.

Step #5 - Select the "Contoured Technique" tab.

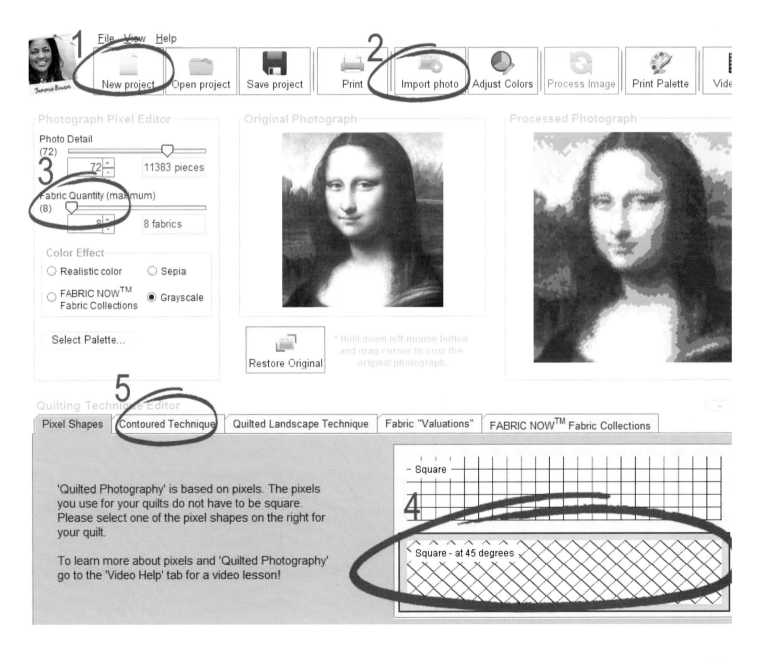

Step #6 - Click "Use this feature"

Step #7 - Use the "Shape Smoothing" slider to merge and contour the pixels. This feature is what creates the magic! Move the slider to the right to merge and smooth the pixels more or to the left to smooth less.

Step #8 - Click "Process Image"

Step #9 - Select "Print" when you are ready to print your pattern.

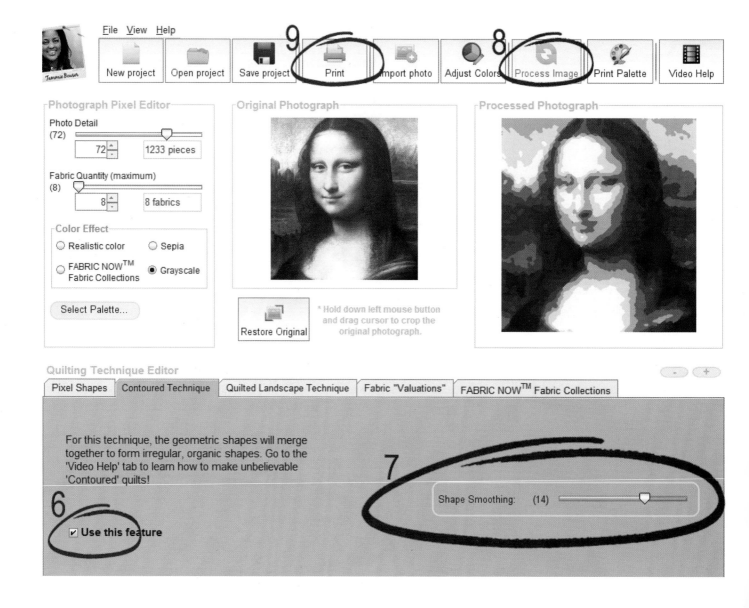

Step #10 - Change the "Size Of Unit" to determine the finished design size. Note: Do not make the unite size smaller than .3 because the printed numbers will be too small to read.

Step #11 - Click "Print Preview" to view your pattern.

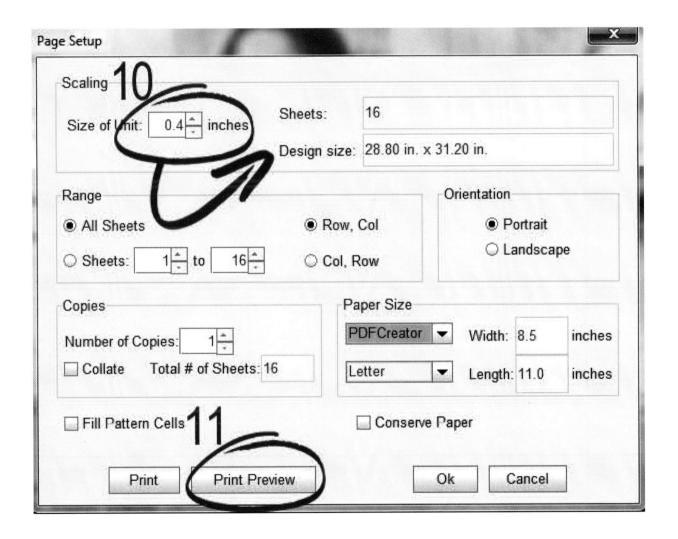

Step #12 - Notice that at the top of each pattern page there are Rows and Columns. These rows and columns will help you put the pattern together in the correct order.

Step #13 - Print your pattern! To put the pages together, cut the excess paper off on one side and match it up to the printing on the next page. Tape the pages together to assemble the complete pattern.

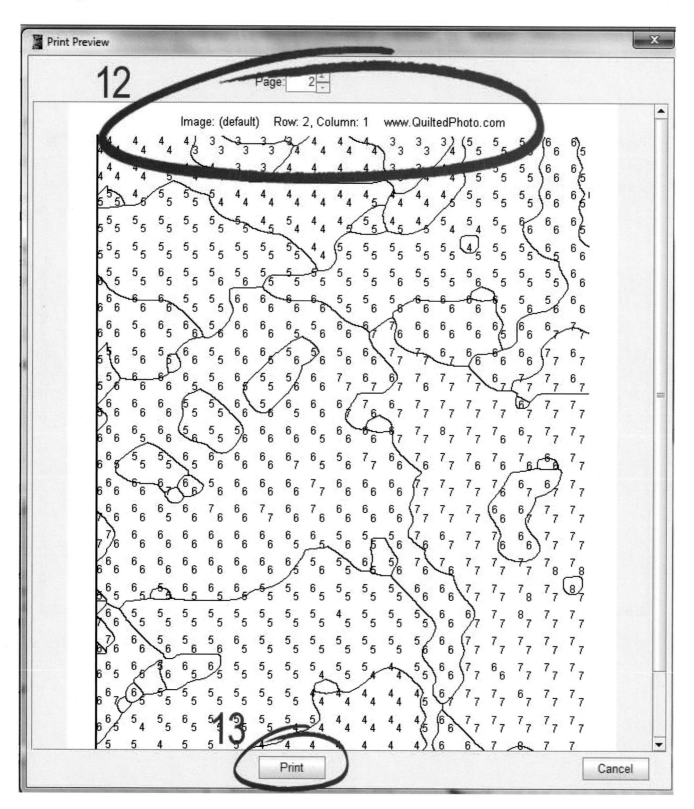

Success Secret #2 - Choose Great Fabric

In this chapter
- Selecting Your Color Palette
- An Easy Way To Choose Colors
- Prints, Patterns or Hand Dyes?
- Pay Attention To Scale
- Notice The Contrast of Scale
- Organizing Your Palette
- Example Of A Great Fabric Palette

To implement the second big **Success Secret**, choose great fabrics! Choosing an intriguing palette of fabric will make your image more than just a carbon copy of the picture... The colors, mix of texture, pattern and scale you apply will transform them into art.

Selecting Your Color Palette
A color palette is a collection of fabrics used for your stiched art project. Choosing the colors for your quilted image is the most creative part of the whole process!

While shopping for your fabric, you may choose any colors you like but your choices will determine the final look of your quilted photo. For example your quilt will have a sophisticated look if you choose muted colors or neutral shades as your color palette. If you select primary colors, or very bright colors, your quilt will have a lively, fun look.

A very important rule to keep in mind while choosing your colors is to stay in one color range. For example, if you have muted shades, choose muted shades for all of your fabrics. Or if you choose bright shades, then choose all bright shades because a fabric that is out of the color range will stand out unattractively.

There are several types of color palettes you can try for choosing your colors I will explain each of them.

Restricted Color Palette
A restricted color palette is a very restricted range of color. This range can have as few as 2 colors. For example you can use pink and purple. While choosing your fabrics, be sure to pick light medium and dark fabrics.

Random Color Palette
A random color palette is made up of fabrics of any color combination. Choosing your color palette at random is fun! I call stitched art made with a random color palette the ultimate scrap quilt! The random color palette is the most surprising type of palette. It really is hard to believe that putting totally unrelated fabrics together can create a beautiful photographic quilt. You could even use all of your favorite fabrics. Once you make a photo quilt with a random color palette, you will understand the importance of color value once and for all.

Single Color Palette
A single color palette is made up of just one color, from the lightest to the darkest shades. This type of palette will work well with any image.

Realistic Color Palette
A realistic color palette is made up of fabric that closely resemble the colors of the original photograph.

The software "Quilted Photo Deluxe" will make realistic color palettes for you.

Remember that you can download a free 7 day trial and make as many patterns as you like for 7 whole days! HowToSewArt.com

Choosing the fabrics for a realistic color palette is the most challenging type of palette to put together. It is more challenging because you will have to consider the colors and values of the fabrics at the same time. This could mean you will have to shop around to find just the right fabrics to match the color palette.

I don't suggest using a realistic color palette for your first project.

An Easy Way To Choose Colors!

Choosing a pleasing fabric selection seems to be the hardest part of the project for some students. I know it can get confusing when you are in the middle of a quilting store surrounded by thousands of fabric bolts! I have been thinking about this problem and I have come up with two surprisingly easy shortcuts that make choosing your fabric palette less of a dilemma.

To use the first shortcut, start by choosing one fabric. I usually pick a colorful middle range fabric. Use the colors in your chosen fabric as a clue for choosing the next fabric. Keep choosing your fabrics with the last fabric as a clue for the next and your palette will have a wonderful, smooth transition from one fabric to the next. Remember that you need light, medium and dark fabrics to create a complete palette. You'll find a video demo for this technique in the free lessons at HowToSewArt.com

For the second shortcut, go to the thread section of your fabric/quilt store. Look at the beautiful variegated threads. You should see a beautiful assortment of cottons, rayons, polyesters and even metallics. They all can be a starting point for choosing your colors. You can use more than one type of thread, for example pick one dark, one medium and one light spool to use together on your project. Variegated threads have fantastic color combination that are already worked out for you, and as an added bonus, the thread will be perfect for quilting your project later!

Prints, Patterns or Hand Dyes?

Wonder what type of fabrics to choose? I like using batik and hand dyed fabrics because of the beautiful painted effect they give my quilts. They look like paint without even trying!

I also really love using printed fabrics and fabrics with over all patterns. Prints create a complex look without adding to the difficulty of the project at all. Printed fabrics will have a totally different end effect than dyed fabrics. Use what you like best!

Here are the three rules you must observe while choosing your fabrics.

Rule #1
Only use fabrics that have a consistent color value. If the fabrics have more than one color, they must be in the same value family. For example if the fabric has light colors, all of the colors in the fabric must be in the light range of color.

Rule #2

Try to avoid prints that have a background that is too highly contrasted. For example a white dot, with a black background would not be suitable because you will not be able to decide on the correct color value. Example A (below) shows a hard to use fabric. Example B is a better choice.

Rule #3

Avoid tie dyed fabrics. They usually have big splotches of highly contrasting colors. Tie dyes are usually not suitable because the color value can change drastically from one area of the yardage to another.

Pay Attention To Scale

Scale is the size of the print, batik or overall pattern of the designs on the fabrics you choose. Try to choose prints or batiks that have a small to medium pattern and that read as a solid if possible. If the size of the pattern is large, different areas of the fabric may have a large variation in value. A large variation in value will make it difficult to sort the fabric by value correctly.

Notice The Contrast of Scale

When I talk about contrasts I am referring to creating visual tension. You add visual tension when each fabric in your palette has a different scale and pattern then all other fabrics in the palette.

Try to have small patterns, medium patterns, solids, something that has a vertical look, maybe a round shape etc. When you look at the whole fabric palette together, each fabric should stand apart because of the variation in color value as well as a variation in the scale of the patterns.

Adding contrast of scale to your fabric palette is one way to make it intriguing to look at!

Organizing Your Palette

After you have chosen your fabrics, organize them by stacking them one on top of the other. Stack them in order from light to dark then pin them all together at the top of the stack. Use stickers to identify each fabric.

Example A

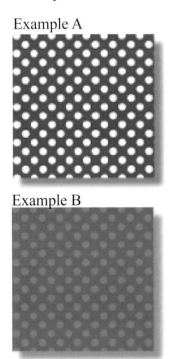

Example B

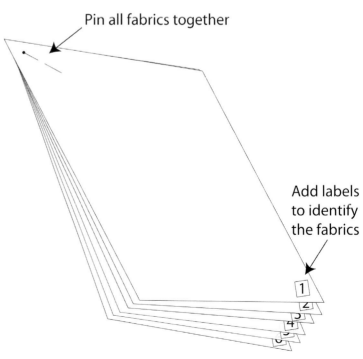

Pin all fabrics together

Add labels to identify the fabrics

Example Of A Great Fabric Palette

This is an example of a great palette. I used this palette for the "Grand Daughters" quilt on page 84.

I followed all of the suggestions for color, scale, pattern and contrast.

These fabrics are from Island Batik Fabrics Spring 2015 Collection
IslandBatik.com

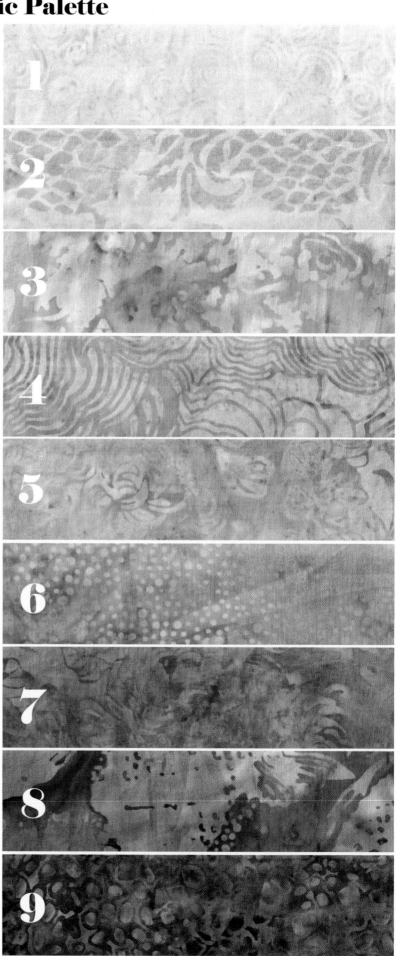

Success Secret #3 - The Magic Contoured Technique!

In this chapter
- Things You'll Need
- Make Your Own Sicky Web
- Putting It Together

Now is the time to teach you the magical, award winning Contoured Pixel™ technique!

Things You'll Need

I will list all of the supplies you will need to make a Magic Contoured Stitched Art project. Each item is followed by a description of the item and how it is used.

Fabrics

I make this style of quilt with 12 fabrics or less. This amount creates an interesting mix of fabrics to look at. See chapter 4 to learn how to choose the best fabric for your project. You will need one quarter yard or less of each fabric. This is a great way to make something really beautiful out of your scraps or your collection of fat quarters.

Variegated Quilting Thread

Since you will be using up to 12 different fabrics ranging from light to dark, I like variegated thread because it has several colors in each spool. This is a great thread to use because you will need a thread that will look good with all of the fabrics. You can use 100% cotton, poly/cotton or rayon thread.

Batting

Batting is the filler in the center of the fabric top and fabric backing. Batting is widely available in polyester, poly/cotton blends and 100% cotton. I prefer 100% cotton batting because it is flat when it is stitched, but use what you prefer. You should be able to find batting at most fabric and craft stores as well as quilting shops.

Fabric For Backing and Binding

You will need to use a fabric for the back as well as the binding around the edges. I use more of one of the fabrics that I included in the top, but you can choose any fabric you like. For the binding, I have found that it is best to use a darker color, because the binding acts as a frame for your stitched image.

Small Scissors

You will need a small pair of scissors with very sharp points. Make sure the scissors are comfortable in your hand. I like the little 5" orange kind...

Basting Spray

The basting spray is a spray adhesive that holds the top, the batting and backing together. The basting spray is an optional item, but I like it because it eliminates the step of basting the three layers together by hand. You should be able to find it at your local fabric/quilt shop or online. It is a great time saver!

Distance Viewer

This is one of my favorite tools! This small scope will let you easily see the photographic image in your stitched art, even close up! It is useful while you are working on the project, and it is fun to use after the stitched art is finished. Each time I work on a new project, I think to myself, "It didn't work this time." Then I look at the finished piece through the distance viewer, and the image just pops out at me! If you plan to make any as gifts, you must give them a distance viewer to go with it! You can get Distance Viewers (door peep holes) at the hardware store for under $5.

Sewing Machine
Your sewing machine should be in good working order, and have the ability to drop the feed dogs.

Free Motion / Darning Foot
This item is also called a quilting foot. If you plan on free motion stitching, you will need a darning foot for your machine. Refer to the documentation for your sewing machine for availability of parts and how to use them.

Flat Work Surface
You will need a flat work surface for placing the fabric shapes. This surface can be a dining table or any other table that is a comfortable height to stand or sit.

Quilting Film / Melt Away Stabilizer
This clear film is applied to the top of your fabric before adding your decrative stitching. You then mark your thread design with a marker! This is like a map for you to follow with your sewing machine! This quilting film is an optional item but I highly recommend it. Watch this video to see
how to use quilting film and where to find it: **HowToSewArt.com/bonus**

Quilted Photo Software or Magic Contoured Pixel™ Patterns
You can make your own custom patterns with Quilted Photo™ Software. Since you purchased this book you can download a fully working trial version of "Quilted Photo Deluxe" for FREE. This FREE trial is really great becasue you can make as many patterns as you want for 7-days! Compatible with Mac and PC.

Go to page 39 to see how easy it is to use the software to make Contoured Pixel™ Patterns from your own photos.

You can also download one free Contoured Pixel™ Pattern when you register for the FREE video lessons.

Sticky Fusible Web or Steam-A-Seam2
Steam A Seam 2 is a sticky fusible webbing with sticky adhesive on both sides (manufactured by The Warm Company). You can find it on rolls at quilt shops. Do not use the lite version of Steam A Seam 2.

You can also make your own sticky web! It is inexpensive to make it yourself and will allow you to make your sticky web in any size you want.

How To Make Your Own Sticky Web

Here are the items you'll need:

1. Parchment Paper - You can easily find it in the grocery store alongside the aluminum foil and plastic wrap. This type of parchment paper is used for baking and is super nonstick.

2. Fusible Web - Fusible web is inexpensive and can be found on a bolt at most fabric or quilt shops.

3. Basting Spray / Craft adhesive spray - This sticky spray can also be found at a quilt shop or craft/art store.

4. Stapler - You can use a normal stapler.

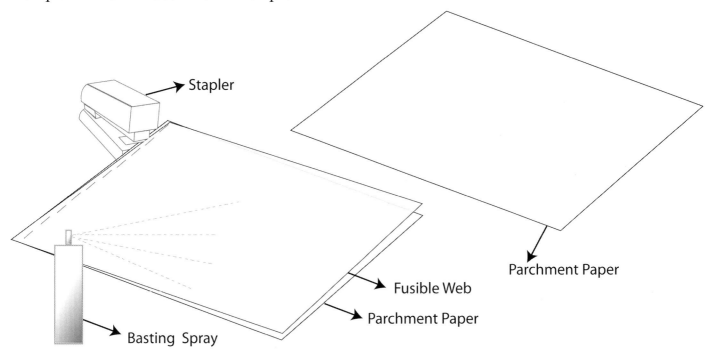

Instructions:

A. Cut a sheet of parchment paper a couple of inches bigger than your pattern (you can staple two sheets of parchment paper together to make a large sheet if necessary).

B. Cut a piece of Fusible Web to match the size of the parchment paper. Staple the top edge of the parchment and fusible web as shown in the image above. You can also staple the bottom edge to keep the layers from moving around.

C. Spray the fusible web with the basting spray. Allow to dry. It should be sticky but not wet. Spray a second layer of basting spray and allow it to dry for a few more minutes.

Now is the time to touch the fusible web with a small piece of fabric to make sure it is sticky enough to hold the fabric securely. If the fabric is not holding securely, spray with another layer of basting spray.

D. To finish your home made sticky web, add another sheet of parchment paper on the top.

Putting It Together

A. To get started, first place your contoured pixel pattern on the table.

B. Peel the back parchment paper off of your sticky web or Steam-A-seam2. Leave the top sheet of parchment paper in place.

C. Place the web on top of your pattern keeping the top parchment paper in place.

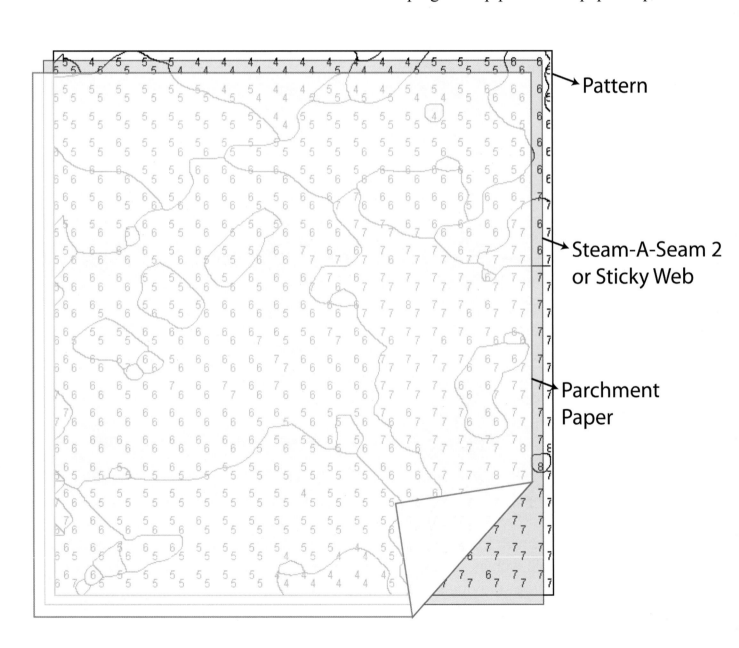

Pattern

Steam-A-Seam 2 or Sticky Web

Parchment Paper

D. Make sure the sticky side of the web is facing up.

E. Sort your fabric palette by color value (from light to dark). Number them with stickers to identify the values. #1 is the lightest, up to the darkest.

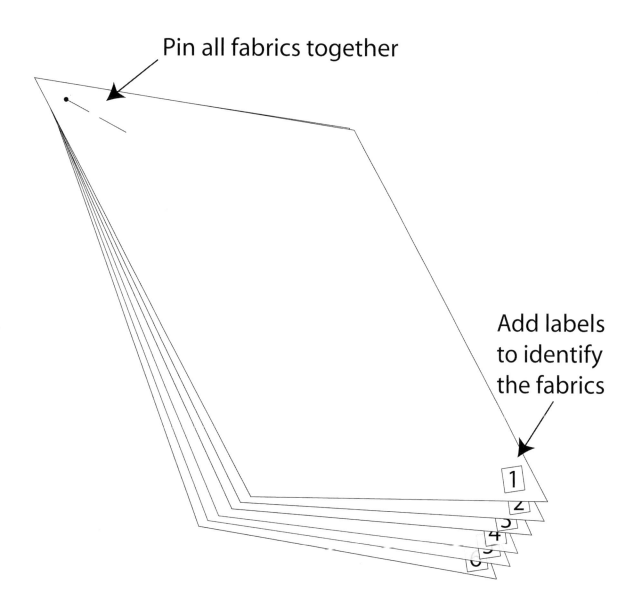

Pin all fabrics together

Add labels
to identify
the fabrics

1
2
3
4
5
6

F. Use a pencil to trace the first contoured shape onto the top paper. Choose a shape that is next to the edge of the pattern. You'll be able to see through the parchment paper.

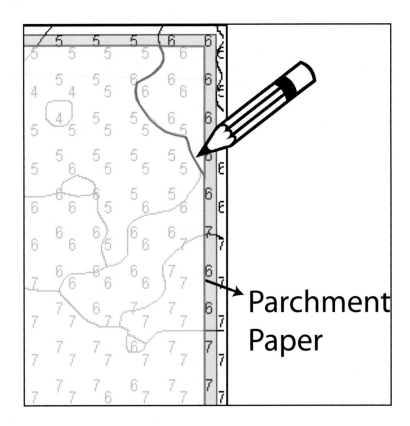

G. Lift up the edge of the parchment paper and cut out the shape. Note: ONLY CUT THE PAPER. NEVER CUT THE STICKY WEB! The paper shape is your pattern piece. You now have an open space exposing the sticky web. This open space is the exact placement for the fabric piece.

H. Use the paper piece you cut as your pattern. The exposed numbers on the pattern tell you what fabric to use. Cut the fabric a little bigger than the pattern (about 1/16th to 1/8th on all sides).

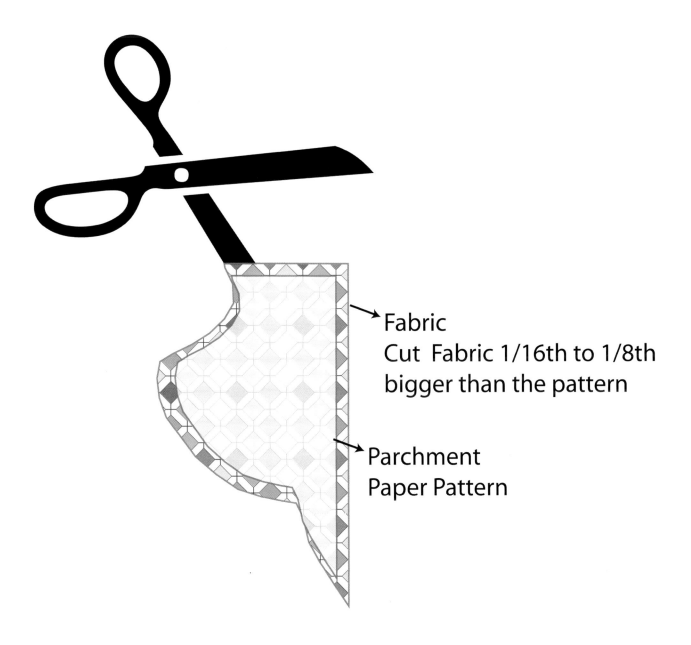

Fabric
Cut Fabric 1/16th to 1/8th
bigger than the pattern

Parchment
Paper Pattern

I. Discard the paper pattern piece then place the contoured fabric on the sticky web with the front side of the fabric facing up. Continue cutting paper pieces one at a time until the whole picture is finished.

J. To finish, peel the numbered paper pattern off the back and place the completed fabric top directly on your batting. Iron the fabric to fuse the contoured fabric pieces onto your batting. Add a backing fabric and stitch to finish. Read the next chapter to learn how to use thread like a paint brush!

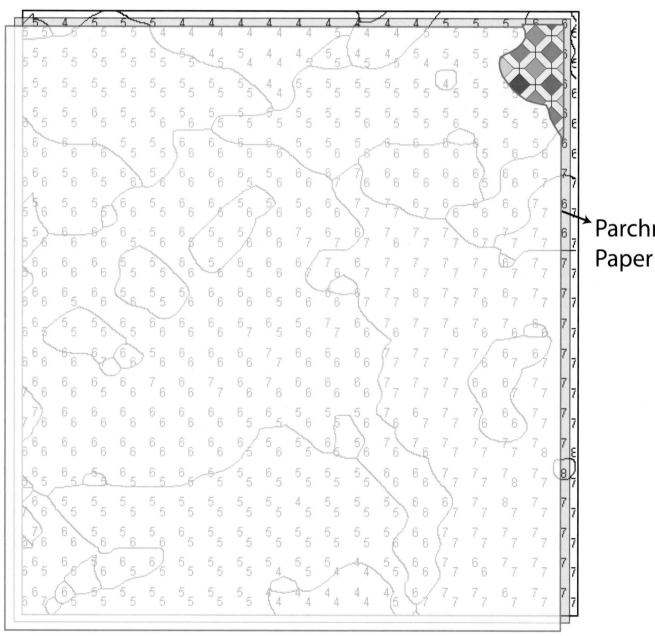

Parchment Paper

Success Secret #4-Use Thread Like A Paint Brush!

In this chapter

The Stitching Adds Texture

The stitching you choose for your stitched art is a layer of texture. The texture is created by the pattern of your stitches. If you compare the stitched art to a painting, think of the stitching as the brush strokes. Thoughtful placement of the stitching can add emphasis to important areas of the image as well.

I will give you some of my ideas about stitching in this chapter. The stitching is also a layer of subtle color, bold contrasting color, or shine. You add this color or shine with the thread you use.

What Thread To Use?

I am in love with variegated threads! They come in 100% cotton, rayons, polyester and metallic. I use them all for different purposes, and I may even use more than one type in the same quilt.

For example, I might use a metallic thread for the light areas of the quilt and a cotton or rayon for the darker areas. I like a lot of stitching and the variegated threads create a more interesting line. A solid color thread would be much to strong and would draw attention away from the image, but the change in the variegated colors keeps your eyes moving around the quilt. It really is a good idea to choose your thread at the beginning of the project. This way you can use the colors in your thread to help you pick your fabrics and also use it to stitch the quilt (see chapter 4 for more details).

Core Concept #8 - Select three threads.
One light variegated, one medium variegated and one dark variegated thread. Stitch on the light fabrics with the light thread, on the medium with the medium thread and the dark with the dark thread. If you follow this core concept, any design you decide to stitch will look good in the end.

Free Motion

Free motion quilting can be either free form or you can follow a pattern.

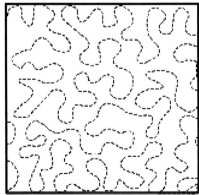
Stipple Quilting Pattern

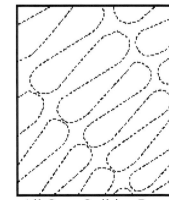
All Over Quilting Pattern

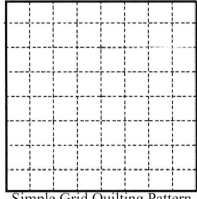
Simple Grid Quilting Pattern

A sample of some all over patterns are a stipple pattern, or a simple all over rounded zig-zag. If you are afraid of free motion you can also try a simple all over pattern like the illustrations on the previous page. The key to simple all over pattern is to get the same amount of stitching over the whole surface.

"Doodlemotion" Stitching

I like to doodle with my sewing machine. This is not thread paintings and it is not embroidery. It is "Doodlemotion" when you follow the contours of your image.

"Doodlemotion" should be very simple graphic shapes. The shapes don't have to be perfect, they just have to follow a general shape or pattern. I really like these gently curving vertical lines. Imagine how this would look with metallic threads!

Try making these gently curving lines with a double or triple needle. The effect will be almost like calligraphy.

Experiment with any stitching shape you like.

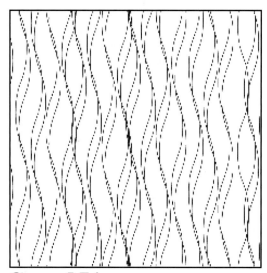

Curved Lines

Core Concept #9 - Use a simple curved stitching pattern to follow along the contours of the image. Stitch a lot of these curved lines and the texture will look like brush strokes!

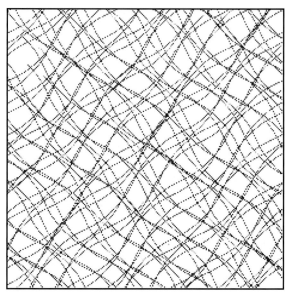

Curved Grid

You can turn the quilt 90 degrees and continue stitching the curved lines to create a grid. This highly stitched pattern will make a great background texture.

Triangle Spirals

Another example of an easy background pattern are these triangle spirals. Remember perfection is not required. Just keep making triangles.

An interesting effect can also be created by changing the stitch setting on your machine to the zig zag stitch. The needle will move back and forth as you move the quilt.

Practicing will make you more skilled at "Doodlemotion" stitching. To do free motion or "Doodlemotion" quilting, you will need to drop the feed dogs of your machine and move the fabric with your hands in any direction. Make sure your body is positioned with the correct posture. The right posture will help you relax so that you can sew the designs with ease. View your video lessons at HowToSewArt.com to see the correct posture.

Embelishments

Metallic threads are so beautiful, but can be difficult to work with because they are more fragile than other threads.

Here are a few tips to keep the threads from breaking so often. The first thing is to use a vertical thread holder for your spool. Second, use a top-stitch or metallic needle.

If you want to add shine without using metalic thread, use Angelina Fiber!

Angelina fiber is simple to use because it is not thread that will break, it is shiny fibers that are as light as air! To use it just sprinkle the fibers where you want the shine then apply "Doodlemotion" on top. Just let the stitching secure the fibers to your stitched art.

Warning: Do not iron over the angelina fiber! If you do, the fibers will melt. My suggestion is to add the angelina fiber as the final step of your sewing.

How To Add The Details

For Core Concept number 8, I told you to stitch on the light fabrics with the light thread, on the medium with the medium thread and the dark with the dark thread. But you can break this rule! I break it when I want to add details to my stitched art!

For example, you will be able to see in the "Grand Daughters" quilt on page 84, I used contrasting thread to change the eye color of the girls to blue. Changing the thread color is an easy way to add details to your stitched art.

How To Sew Your Signature

To finish off your stitched art, you must add your signature. You can add a label to the back side of the quilt if you prefer but I always stitch my signature with thread right on the front. It is easy and this is how to do it.

To make stitching my name easy, I use Quilting Film. Quilting Film is a clear film that looks like plastic, but it is a special kind of clear "plastic" film. You can use a permanent marker to sign your signature on the film then place your signature exactly where you want it. Placement is easy because you can see through the clear film.

Use a glue stick to apply the small piece of film with your signature in the location you have decided. I always place my signature in the lower right area of the stitched art.

The next step is to use your free motion or "Doodlemotion" skills to stitch your signature! Be sure to use a solid colored, contrasting thread for stitching your signature so that it will be easily visible. It is also a good idea to stitch over your signature twice to make sure it is visible.

After you finish sewing, tear away the excess film around your stitching.

Now get an iron set on the highest setting. Iron your stitched signature with pressure in a circular motion and all of the film will shrink into small hard balls that will easily brush away. It will not harm your iron I promise! You will have a beautiful stitched signature!

View my video demonstration at: HowToSewArt.com/bonus

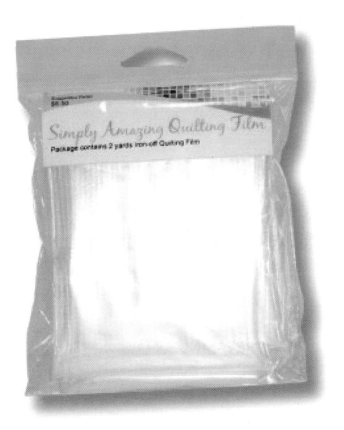

What kind sewing machine do you have? I own and use a normal home sewing machine. I used a Janome 6500 to stitch most of the quilts in this book. But I have always been intrested in trying a long arm quilting machine... and I finally got the chance!

While working at a quilt show in the spring of 2014, a wonderful lady named Jenny stepped into my booth. After talking to her for a while about her philanthropy and community service work, I realized that I had met her years before at the beginning of my quilting career. As our conversation continued, she told me about her long arm quilting machines and that she gives lessons! What a blessing!

I did take Jenny's long arm lessons and stitched three of my Contoured Pixel™ Quilts very quickly and I love it! I stitched "Grand Daughters", "Tree Trunk" and "Trumpet". You can see the beautiful stitching in the "Stitched Art Gallery" and on my website. Free motion quilting or "Doodlemotion" quilting is great on a regular sewing machine but it is faster and easier on a Long Arm. If you are in Southern California and want to rent sewing time on a Gammill Classic Long Arm, I recommend that you visit Jenny at: **www.PatchesFabrics.com**

Boothill "Patches" Fabrics
9749 Mason Avenue
Chatsworth, CA 91311
(818) 709-2678

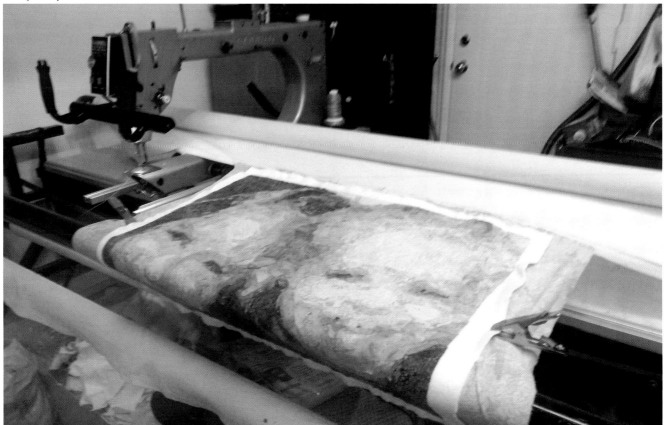

#52686541

How To Sew Art Quiz #3

What Are The 2 Core Concepts We Discussed In This Chapter?

Core Concept #8 _____

_____

Core Concept #9 _____

_____

Finishing Your Art Masterpiece!

In this chapter
- Trimming The Edges
- How To Add A Border
- Add A Traditional Binding
- Add A Modern Invisible Binding
- How To Add A Display Sleeve

Even though you have stitched, signed and embelished your amazing stitched art, the project is not complete until you have made it suitable for display. There are many ways you can finish your quilt top. I will discuss each of the available options in this chapter. The options range from borders, to bindings, to adding a sleeve to hang it on the wall.

Trimming The Edges

If you have fused your pieces perfectly inside the lines, your quilt will finish with perfectly straight edges and squared corners. However when you add the stitching the shape will become uneven and require trimming.

Use a rotary cutter and mat to trim off any uneven edges. Make sure it is squared and even so that your stitched art hangs level when displayed on a wall.

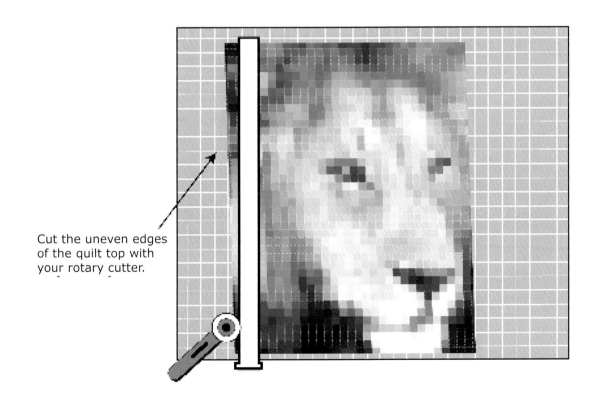

Cut the uneven edges of the quilt top with your rotary cutter.

How To Add A Border

A border is a straight strip of fabric sewn around the edges of your quilt to frame it.

A border can make your photo quilt even more beautiful but borders also have a practical purpose. Adding a border will make the edges of the quilt perfectly straight, and the corners will be perfectly squared. The border will make your stitch art hang perfectly straight on the wall without any wavy edges. Another added bonus is that the border will increase the size of the quilt and provide another place to put decorative stitching.

Adding a border is a decision you will make after you see the finished quilt top. You can add one or two borders or have no border at all.

When you think about adding borders to your quilted photos, you can pretend you are adding a matting and frame. Pay attention to the way paper photographs are framed. Also look at how paintings and other works of art are finished. Notice how the colors relate to the art work, and pay close attention to the proportion of the border in relation to the art work. There are two types of borders - straight cut borders and mitered borders. I will explain both types.

To add a border, the first step is to measure at the center of the quilt in both directions. Be sure to measure in the center of the quilt because the edges of the quilt are probably stretched and

Diagram A - Straight Border

Diagram B - Mitered Border

are not accurate. The center measurements will determine what length to cut the border strips. Cut the border strips across the width of the fabric.

Straight Border

A straight border has straight seams on the corners. See diagram A on page 62. To add a straight border, the first step is to measure the center horizontally. Cut two border strips this exact length. Stitch the borders to the sides, easing the top to match the border if it is necessary.

Next measure the center in the vertical direction including the border that you just applied. Cut two border strips that exact length. Stitch the border easing the two together if it is necessary. If you want a second straight border, repeat this process.

Mitered Border

A mitered border is a border with diagonal seam on the corners. See diagram B on page 62.

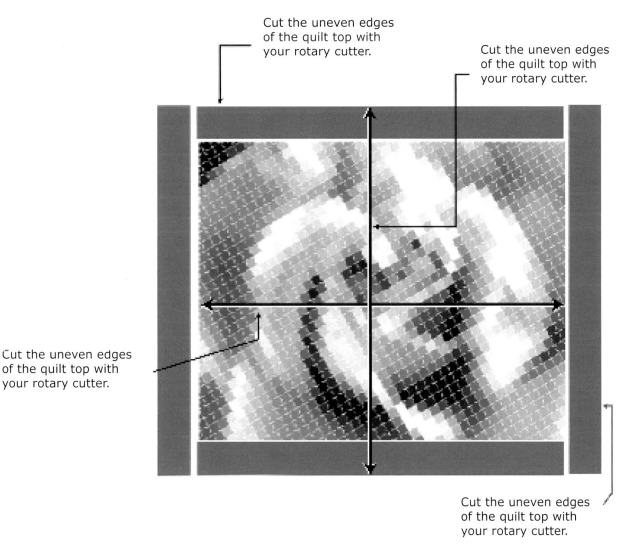

Cut the uneven edges of the quilt top with your rotary cutter.

Cut the uneven edges of the quilt top with your rotary cutter.

Cut the uneven edges of the quilt top with your rotary cutter.

Cut the uneven edges of the quilt top with your rotary cutter.

To add a mitered border, first measure the center in the vertical direction. Next measure the width of the border. Now cut two border strips the vertical length + the width of the border times 2.

Mark the width of the border on each end of the border pieces. Cut the corners as shown in the diagram below. Cut from the outside corner, down to the border marks. Stitch the border pieces to the sides, easing the top into

the border if it is necessary. Stop your stitching 1/4" from the edge. Repeat these steps for the horizontal edges.

To Create The Corner Seams
Fold the quilt in half diagonally so that the ends of the border meet (see diagram on next page). Stitch the corner seams with 1/4" seam allowances. Repeat this step for all four corners.

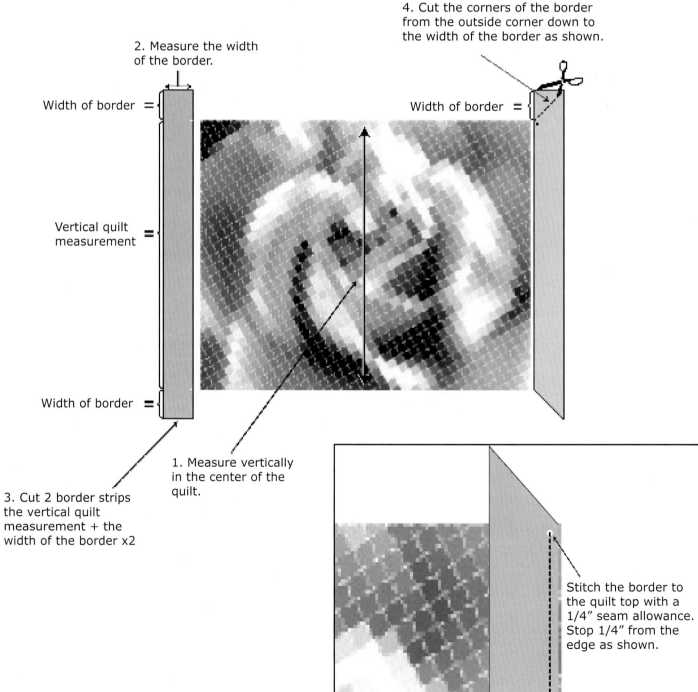

4. Cut the corners of the border from the outside corner down to the width of the border as shown.

2. Measure the width of the border.

Width of border =

Width of border =

Vertical quilt measurement =

Width of border =

1. Measure vertically in the center of the quilt.

3. Cut 2 border strips the vertical quilt measurement + the width of the border x2

Stitch the border to the quilt top with a 1/4" seam allowance. Stop 1/4" from the edge as shown.

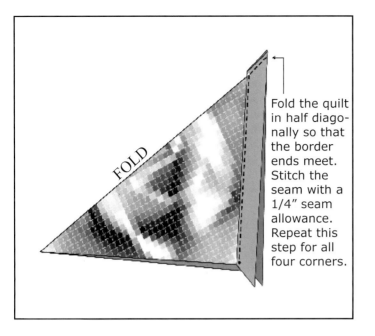

Fold the quilt in half diagonally so that the border ends meet. Stitch the seam with a 1/4" seam allowance. Repeat this step for all four corners.

FOLD

Important: If you are going to add a border, you must add it before you add your stitching.

Basting stitched through the quilt sandwich.

Quilt Top

Backing

Batting

Bindings

After the quilting is finished, you still need to finish the edges. You will finish the edges with a binding and I will show you how to make two different types. The first type of binding is a classic binding and the second type is an invisible binding.

Add A Traditional Binding

A classic binding will make a 1/4" edge around the outside. To make a classic binding, the first thing you will do is cut strips 1 1/2" wide. Cut the strips across the width of the fabric. Stitch the strips together to form one long strip as shown in diagram A.

Diagram A

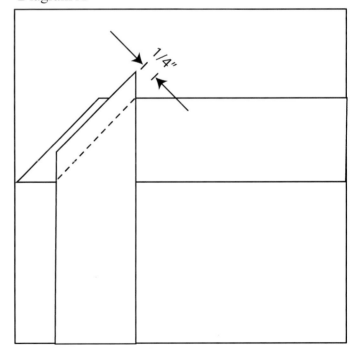

1/4"

Fold the binding strip in half the long way, and then place the binding on the front of the quilt with the raw edges together. Stitch the binding with a ¼" seam as shown in diagram B.

Diagram B

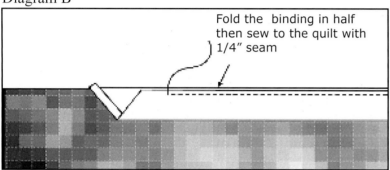

Fold the binding in half then sew to the quilt with 1/4" seam

To continue the binding around the corner, stop stitching ¼" from the edge.

Diagram C

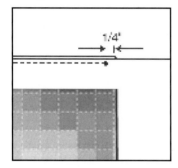

1/4"

Fold the binding upward, creating an angled corner as shown in diagram D.

Diagram D

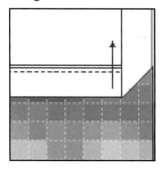

Then fold the binding back downward (creating a squared corner), leaving a fold of fabric as shown. Pin the fold in place and stitch the next side of the binding. You can begin stitching from the corner edge.

Diagram E

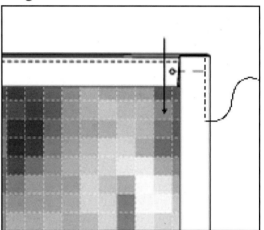

The next step is to wrap the binding around the quilt edge, then over to the back as shown in diagram F. The last step is to stitch the edge of the binding in place with a small whipstitch.

Diagram F

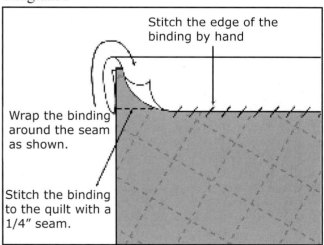

Stitch the edge of the binding by hand

Wrap the binding around the seam as shown.

Stitch the binding to the quilt with a 1/4" seam.

Add A Modern Invisible Binding

An invisible binding will not show at all when viewing the stitched art from the front. To make an invisible binding, the first thing you will do is cut strips 1 1/2" wide. Fold the binding strip in half, and then place the binding on the front with the raw edges together. Stitch the binding with a 1/4" seam allowance as shown in diagram B on page 66.

After stitching the binding all the way around, fold the binding and the seam upward, and away from the quilt. Stitch the binding 1/8" away from the seam as shown in the diagram below. This stitch will force the binding and the seam allowance to roll towards the backside.

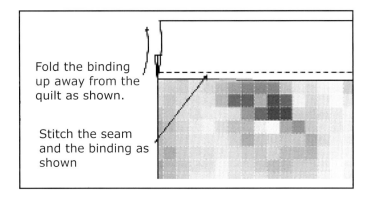

Fold the binding up away from the quilt as shown.

Stitch the seam and the binding as shown

The last step is to stitch the edge of the binding in place with a small whipstitch.

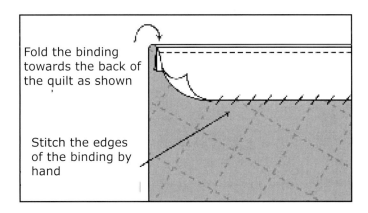

Fold the binding towards the back of the quilt as shown

Stitch the edges of the binding by hand

How To Add A Display Sleeve

When you prepare to display your stitched art, you first need to think about how to care for it. Since these projects are intended to be art that is hung on a wall, you should not have to worry about them getting dirty. However you will need to remove dust from time to time if they are not framed behind glass. To remove the dust, just put the quilt in a cool clothes dryer for 10 minutes. The dryer will remove the dust without damaging the your hard work.

After you have learned how to care for your stitched art, you must decide how you will display it. The most obvious way is to have it framed professionally.

The way that I prefer to display my Contoured Pixel™ Art is to add a sleeve to the back as shown in the diagram on the next page. To add the sleeve, just make a 4" fabric tube the width of the stitched art. Then hand stitch the fabric tube on the top as shown in the diagram on the next page. To hang the quilt you will need a cafe curtain rod. Apply the curtain rod to the wall according to the manufacturer's instructions. Pull the curtain rod through the sleeve to hang your masterpiece. You can buy cafe curtain rods at any hardware store

Curtain rod

Stitch a 4" tube on the back of the quilt. Stitch the tube by hand on the top and the bottom as shown.

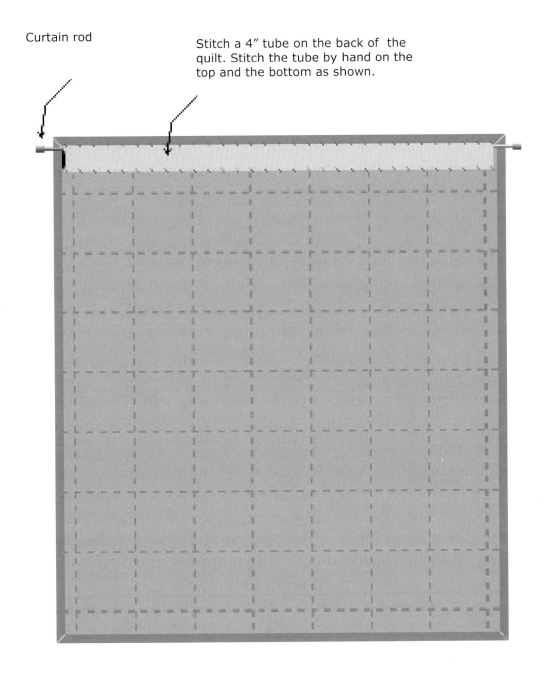

Making A Profit

In this chapter
- Selling Your Stitched Art!
- Who Is Your Client?
- Setting Your Prices
- Promoting your work
- Other Ways To Profit
- Last Minute Suggestions

Selling Your Stitched Art!

Before you're ready to start selling.......you need to know much more than just how to sew! You must be prepared with the right frame of mind about all the non-sewing parts of being an artist..

Imagine this: you've been sitting at your desk ordering business cards and working on your website for weeks and weeks. After spending lots of money you're finally finish. You're excited about your new business, so you wait... and wait but customers do not arrive.

If this is your story then chances are that your do not have an effective plan and you're spending your time on the wrong priorities.

Who Is Your Client?

Before you can make an effective business plan, you must choose your ideal customer.

You should choose potential clients that have an irrational passion. Good examples of irrational passions would include pet owners, new grand parents or people with collections of expensive cars.

Once you choose your ideal client, it's important to do some basic market research. The reaserch will help you define your target before you start devoting your resources (time, money, talent) to the project. This will save you a lot of time and frustration.

One good way of doing this is to create a checklist of questions that must be answered before you undertake your project. Here is an example of a checklist I would use:

☑ **Who will buy my stitched art?**

☑ **Is my art really wanted? (is there demand)**

☑ **How large is the market?**

☑ **How will I reach these people and convince them to buy?**

☑ **Can this market be tested?**

☑ **Is anyone else selling similar art?**

☑ **What makes my stitched art stand out from the rest?**

☑ **Can I sell my art and make a profit?**

☑ **How much time, effort and money will have to be put into each piece to be profitable?**

☑ **Do I have the energy, resources and drive to build an ongoing business?**

Once you have completed your basic market

research and answered all the questions, then you can start formulating a marketing strategy.

Your work will be a lot easier if you've objectively answered the questions. Ignoring this process is almost a sure way to fail in business. Without knowing the answers there is no way to target your client.

The next thing you'll need to understand is your potential clients motivations. What is it that gets them excited?

Arousing the emotions and desires of your potential clients plays a major role in your success. You must learn to arouse your customers' emotions and desires.

New businesses waste millions of dollars yearly because they don't understand that what they want to sell and what the customer wants to buy may be two different things. But you will find success if you can find a way to appeal to their desires and emotions with your art.

Emotions are what drive people to buy things. Moving the prospect to buy should be the sole purpose of your marketing. You'll need to stir up enough emotions to cause desire. Actually, they need to have enough desire to cause them to logically rationalize buying your art.

Remember that most people's actions are caused by instincts and impulses that they are unaware of.

When choosing your marketing angle, try to understand how your art might appeal emotionally to potential clients. You can do this by putting yourself in their shoes while focusing on your own feelings. Always be planning a way to arouse a clients emotions and desires. This should be easy because you've already done your research and you know a lot about your potential clients!

Setting Your Prices

Another key reason to research your customer is that you can then match your selling prices within the average price range of stitched art offered to your targeted segment of the market. For example, promoting your work for $300 in a location that features art for $50, probably won't be effective.

For this reason, it is a good idea to also consider the location of the promotion when selecting the particluar works to present. If you display things on Etsy.com, perhaps you will have smaller things with a lower price or bigger, more expensive items can be displayed when you are at a gallery, art fair or trade show. What kind of merchandise would you display at a pet shop, car show or horse show?

Another strategy would be to always work on developing a distinctive style or a signature look. Your style will become recognized and sought out by collectors. You can claim a destinct look by only using a certian type of fabric, only using bright colors or maybe innovative dog portraits! Over time, your signature look will add value to your work.

A good habit to keep is to always write down the time you spend working on each project. To correctly determine the price of each piece, you should also keep track of the cost of the materials you use. However, time is by far the biggest portion of the price.

Some artists figure their prices by the square inch but you will have to keep track of your time for a while to find out what your square inch price should be.

I also suggest that you include some items that are small and quick to make in your line up. You will also need samples of larger (higher priced) "WOW" pieces to capture attention.

Once you know how many hours you've used, multiply the hours by your hourly rate. Your hourly rate will go up as your reputation grows and as the demand for your work increases.

The bottom line is that time matters and you must pay attention to it if you want to be profitable.

Promoting Your Work

Are you uneasy about promoting your work? Do you have negative ideas about being a salesman? You have to get over this because it all comes down to whether you want to end up being another broke artist or if you want to sell your art and enjoy all the benefits.

The key to your success depends on how visible you are to your target customers! This includes print advertising, art show displays, online ads and even bulletin boards at your local quilt shop. Constant promotion is the only way to get your art out to the public. You have to know how to effectively advertise or your ideas and efforts will be wasted.

Your art and your marketing has to be original. It has to be different and stand apart from the rest, especially when you have other artists competing for the same customer. If you and your work stand out, you will have a chance at being remembered.

The most important things to remember about marketing your work is to design your promotions to attract your target audience, try to be visible to your audience continually and be original so that you stand out from the rest.

Other Ways To Profit

You've just learned how to start selling your stitched art but here is another way to profit from Contoured Pixel™ Art. You can teach Stitched Art classes to others. You can teach at quilt shops, fabric shops, quilt guilds as well as American Sewing Guild meetings.

To be a teacher of Contoured Pixel™ Art you'll need to be certified as a teacher. Teaching is how I started making a living from my work and I am still a teacher now!

I have also prepared a "Teacher's Guide Book" to guide you. It contains forms, tips for getting full classes, student handouts, class outlines, check lists and all of the profit building tools you'll need to handle a class full of students.

The "Teacher's Guide Book" is included when you enroll in the Teachers' Certification Home Study Course. See page 74 for details.

Another way to profit is to promote this book and software! You can promote via email, online or in your classroom.

Each time a person buys the software using your private link, you will get a portion of the sale. Promoting Stitched Art products is a perfect way to boost your earnings from teaching because you will be promoting to people who are 100% interested in Stitched Art.

You will get a seller's account when you are certified as my Contoured Pixel™ Art teacher. See page 74 for details.

Last Minute Suggestions

Being an artist requires that you spend a considerable amount of time developing your own distinctive artistic style as well as time building your reputation. The problem is that this journey is usually spent alone. It's much easier to remain productive and always moving towards success when you're surrounded by people who are on the same journey.

What if you could join a community to solve the problem? Well you can! I've set up a community based on positivity and mutual support. Now you and other artists can support each other online!

Staying focused on the right priorities is much easier when you have access to other stitched artists that also have the desire to achieve success.

This community's goal is to empower each member along their pathway to success.

Now what? Come join us at:
HowToSewArt.com

Now it's time to get started!

Become a Certified Teacher!
Learn all the techniques and how to teach them to students!

These students are happy because they made these personalized quilted photos in an easy 4 hour class! The secrets of a successful class like this are contained within this course. I will teach you the techniques. You'll learn how to structure the classes for maximum profit, plus you get the exact handouts, flip chart and documents I use. When you have completed the course, you'll get the required certification to teach 4 amazing techniques!

Teacher's Certification Course– $447

This certification course includes all of the video courses below as well as exclusive teachers lessons. You'll get a teachers guide book, personalized guidance from Tammie and an official certificate authorizing you to teach these 4 proprietary techniques.

Simply Amazing Quilted Photography

Learn how to make a pixel quilt with pieced squares. You will learn how to make quilts like the ones in my first book "Simply Amazing Quilted Photography". Each pixel quilt takes only a short time to make and you'll learn the simple sewing technique that will reduce your sewing time by 85%. The quilts look intricate and difficult to make, but it's easy…even if you are just beginning to sew.

More Amazing Quilted Photography

Learn to transform ordinary fabric strips n' pieces into unbelievably beautiful photographic quilts!   In this course you will learn how to make your photo quilts look more painted and less digital. Your friends will be amazed when they realize your quilt is really a photograph! As seen on Friends of Kaye on PBS, and Sewing With Nancy on PBS. One of Tammie's quilts made with this technique was bought by the Shelbourn Museum in 2011. This course is all inclusive and includes fabric!

Doodlemotion...Free Motion The Easy Way!

In this course, we will explore Free Motion Quilting and how I do it. I call it doodlemotion because it feels like doodling when you get the hang of it.

Magical Contoured Pixel™

You'll learn how to do this amazing contoured technique. This course will allow you to make quilts that are ART… they catch the attention of all who see them. Even rock stars! My student Jean took the class and her quilt caught the eye of Rod Stewart himself! He even let her go back stage at his concert! Tammie also won the attention of the judges at Quilt National '07 and won the Japan Award!

Doodle Art Quilts

This fun course teaches you how to make amazing quilts using drawings or even paintings. Make quilts from your children's or grandchildren's drawings. These cute quilts will keep them warm and will be a keepsake forever reminding them of when they were small.

Making A Profit With Stitched Art

Are you ready to start making a profit with your stitched art? This video course will show you how to turn your art into cash.
You'll learn how to find clients, how to promote your work and a strategy for setting your prices. Includes a special video about how to use social media in your marketing.

Gallery Of Contoured Pixel™ Art

"Marley"

This amazing piece was made as a commissioned work for a client. It was so beautiful that I really wanted to keep it for myself! I used many different stitching formations to create lots of contrasting textures.

"Duke"

I wanted to create a sepia effect and even though the fabrics have many colors, the overall effect is sepia. My great uncle Jim Taylor was an amazing photographer and took this photo at the Montery Jazz Festival in the 50's. I displayed this quilt at Smithsonian Craft Show when I was invited as a juried artist.

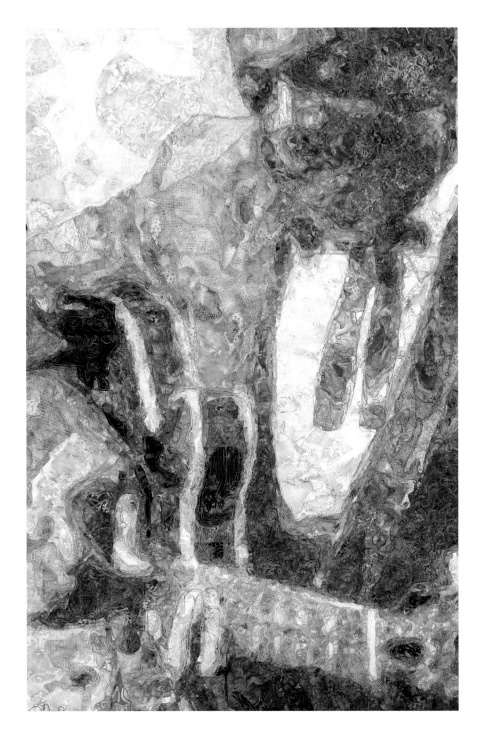

"Lucille"

This is the image of BB King as a young man. I experimented with color and shine. I used hot pink, orange and pastels and I really love it! I also highlighted the neck of the guitar with shiny silver angelina fiber to make "Lucille" the main focus. The picture was taken by my uncle Jim Taylor and this piece was displayed at the Smithsonian Craft Show.

"Shroud"

I like to do some kind of experiment for each new project that I make. For this one, I stitched the whole thing with little loops and spirals. I didn't know if it would be effective, but it is!

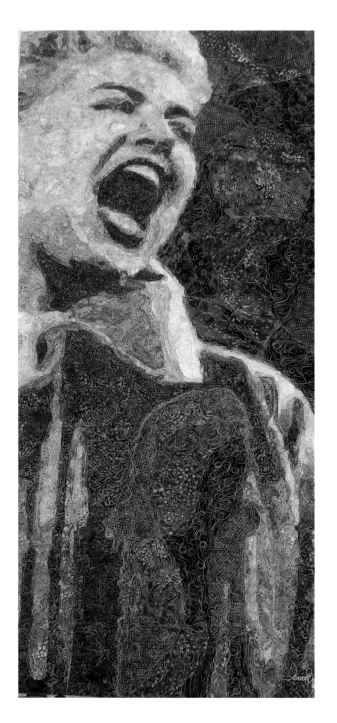

"Song"

I am proud of this work because it was displayed in the book "500 Art Quilts: An Inspiring Collection of Contemporary Work". My quilts were selected by Karey Bresenhan from Quilts, Inc. Karey is one of the most prominent figures in quilting.

It was the winner of the Japan award for Quilt National in 2007. It was also displayed at the Smithsonian Craft Show.

"Jazz Trombone"

I am proud of this Stitched Art piece because it was displayed in the book "500 Art Quilts: An Inspiring Collection of Contemporary Work". My quilts were selected by Karey Bresenhan from Quilts, Inc. Karey is one of the most prominent figures in quilting.

It was also displayed at the Smithsonian Craft Show. The photograph was taken by my great uncle Jim Taylor at the Montery Jazz Festival in the 50's.

Free "Gerber Daisey" Contoured Pattern

This flower became stunning stitched art and only has 6 fabrics. After purchasing this book you can download the pattern when you register for the online video class. **HowToSewArt.com**

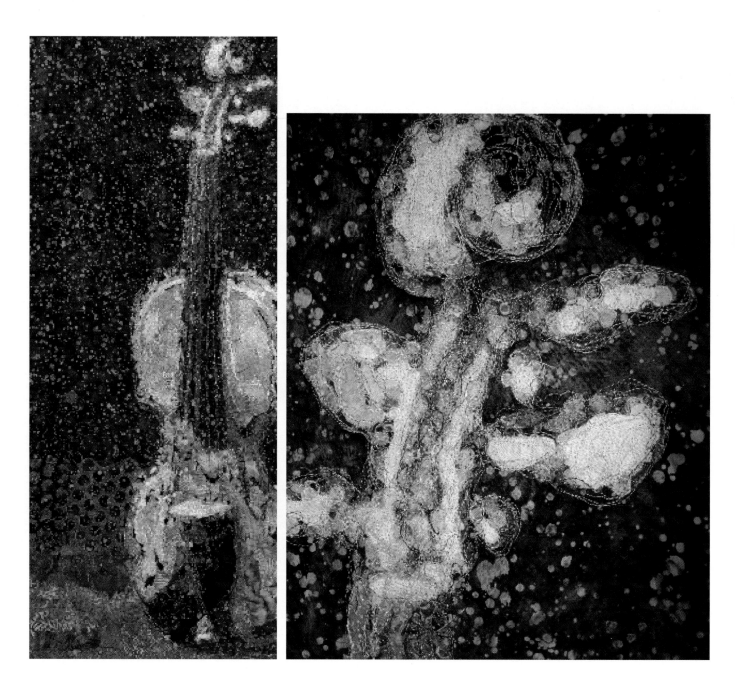

"Violin"

This work was created as a gift for my Quilt National friends in Japan! When I won the Japan award in 2007, I also won a trip to Japan. I gave this quilt to the sponsor of my award (Nihon Vogue Corporation) as a way to show my appreciation for the awesome award and amazing experience.

"Mom"

I made this portrait for my friend Sue Ann Taylor. It is a really clear example of using thread like a paint brush! I used "Doodlemotion" stitching to create texture and movement. Sue Ann Taylor is the founder of Quilters News Network.

"Grand Daughters"

With this project I wanted to use colorful and happy fabrics because the girls are so happy! I used a photo of Nancy's grandaughters to be featured on the PBS show "Sewing With Nancy". Notice that I added details by stitching their eyes with blue thread to make sure the girls eyes are blue in the finished Stitched Art. I used the Gammill Classic long arm machine to add the stitching.

"Joyful"

I am always amazed at how easy it is to capture the emotion in someone's face in fabric! I love this work because the musician is so "Joyful". My great uncle Jim Taylor took this photo at the Montery Jazz Festival. It was displayed at the Smithsonian Craft Show when I was invited as a juried artist.

"Trumpet"

For this trumpet I decided to make an interesting background of large bubbles contrasted against highly textured small bubbles. I used the Gammill Classic long arm machine to add the stitching.

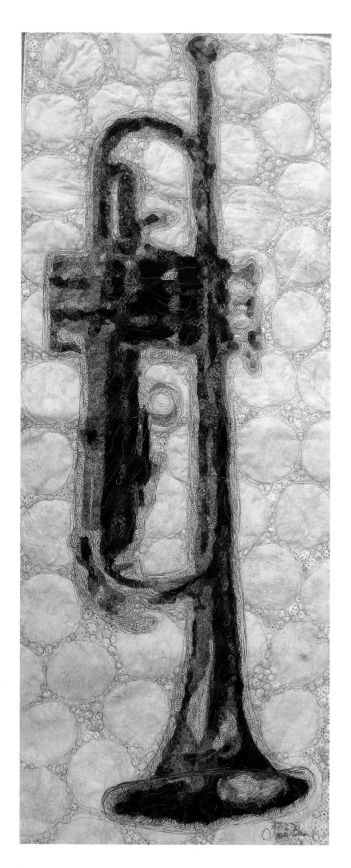

456811

"Tree Trunk"

In the original photo the background had random people, bushes etc.
I decided to simplify the background and remove all of the irrelevant
things in the background. I did that in order to keep all of the focus on the
beautiful tree trunk. I used the Gammill Classic long arm machine to add the
stitching.

Conclusion

My goal has been to teach you how to sew your own amazing Contoured Pixel™ stitched art. I hope you agree that I have reached my goal!

When you visit my website I will also share my new ideas, offer exclusive student discounts, and I may even invite you to contribute to my next book!

Will you share your success with me? I would like to see your stitched art and I really want to hear your comments. If you want join the conversation on social media use hashtag **#SewArt** on Facebook and Twitter.

To send your photos and comments visit me at: www.**TammieBowser.com**

Want to join me on Facebook? I'm giving away a FREE fabric palette every month! The beautiful fabrics are selected by me and sorted by color value... exactly like I've taught you in this book! Come join the fun at: **www.Facebook.com/QuiltFabric**

Before I finish, I want to give sepcial thanks to Island Batik for the beautiful hand dyed fabrics! All of the new quilts for this book were made with fabrics from the Island Batik Spring 2015 collection. Go to **IslandBatik.com** to see the amazing fabrics and to find a local retailer.

"Valuations" on your iPhone for FREE
from Mosaic Quilt Studio... No Strings Attached!

You can download a "lite" version of the Color Valuations application for your iPhone or iPad. IT'S FREE! Now you can and carry the powerful value sorting software with you to the fabric store or anywhere!

"Lite" and "Pro" versions now available in the App Store

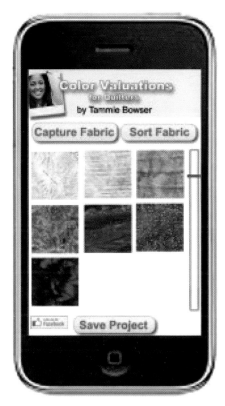

Get video lessons on your phone!

Scan this QR code

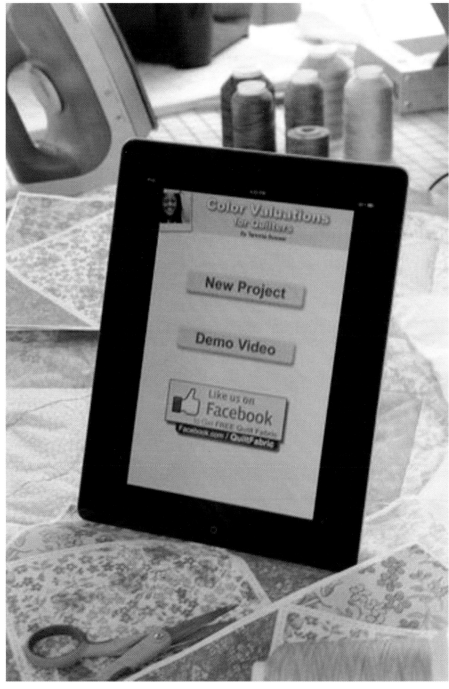

Or text the word: colorvalue to (818) 6263 - SEW
(739)
Visit the HowToSewArt.com for more details.

Sort Your Fabric With My "Value Isolation" Method

1. Choose your fabric selection. Include light, medium and dark fabrics.

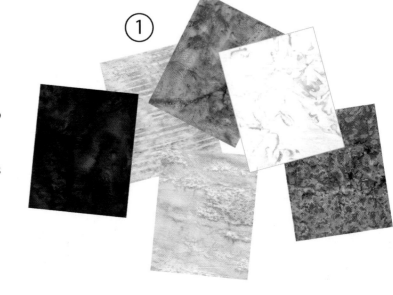

2. Line them up from light to dark the best you can. Do not work to hard or spend to much time sorting your fabrics because we will use the "Value Isolation Tool" to double check the order and adjust them.

3. Place the value isolation tool over the first two fabrics with one hole over each fabric. The only thing you need to ask yourself is if the second fabric is darker then the first!

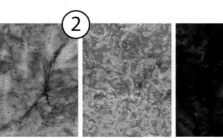

4. If the answer is yes, then you continue by placing the tool over the next two fabrics. If the answer is no, then you move the fabric to find the correct placement.

5. Use the tool to view all of the fabrics. Continue until the fabrics are in order from the lightest to darkest!

You can get a "Value Isolation Tool" for yourself if you pay the shipping at HowToSewArt.com or get one free with any other product order.

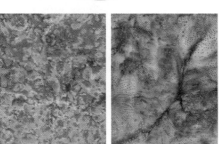

Tools And Materials You Will Need

How To Sew Art Book

Learn the magical Contoured Pixel™ technique Tammie used to win awards! This book is inspiring and will teach you the secrets for becoming a real artist! It is used as the text book for the "Magical Contoured Pixel™ Video Course".

★★★★★ ☑ (4)

#1 Best Seller ‹ in Sewing

Books: See all 8 items

Simply Amazing Quilted Photography

You can make simple pixel quilts easily when you know the secrets! This book is a classic and a best-seller...a MUST HAVE! It is used as the text book for the Simply Amazing Quilted Photography home study course. Printed Books and Kindle Books available.

More Amazing Quilted Photography

You can make amazing quilted art easily with the innovative applique technique! The ballerina quilt on the cover was purchased by Shelburne Museum in Vermont. You'll learn how to make pixel quilts that look less digital! This book is a MUST HAVE! It is used as the text book for the More Amazing Quilted Photography home study course. Printed Books and Kindle Books available.

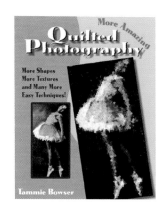

Amazing Chenilled Quilted Photography

You'll learn how to make photo quilts with texture! This book will teach you how to make amazing furry animal quilts and more. If you have any of the other Quilted Photography books, then this book will be an amazing addition to your collection. Printed Books and Kindle Books available.

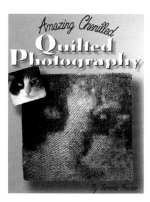

Stitch-A-Sketch 1.0

You want basic and economical art quilt software? Well Stitch-A-Sketch 1.0 is what you need. This program is part of a family of software programs made specially for art quilting. This software make the Magic Contoured Pixel™ patterns you learned about in this book without all of the extra bells and whistles.

The new software includes design options for grayscale or realistic fabric palettes. You can also print a shopping design sheet that tells you how much of each material you will need and finished quilt size and more. The most exciting and time saving new feature is the full size printing feature! Stitch-A-Sketch also contains all of the functions of "Valuations" software at no extra charge! Just tape the patterns pages together, and you will be ready to start!

Retail Price $99.95

Quilted Photo Deluxe 2.0

Want advanced Art Quilt features? well here it is! You can make the kind of quilts you learned about in this book and you will make all of the styles of patterns from all of my books! Quilted Photo Deluxe 2.0 has 16 new pixel shapes, basic square pixel patterns, paper piecing patterns and you can automatically design the Magical Contoured Pixel™ patterns! This is the technique I used to design the winning art quilts in this book!! Quilted Photo Deluxe 2.0 is the best art quilt software in the world. It is easy to use and reliable. This program is part of a family of software programs made specially for art quilts.

Includes options for grayscale or realistic color palettes. You can also print a shopping design sheet that tells you how much of each fabric you will need, finished quilt dimensions and more. The most time saving feature is the full size printing feature! Quilted Photo Deluxe also contains all of the functions of "Valuations" software at no extra charge! Just tape the pattern pages together, and you will be ready to start!

Features & Benefits Of QPD 2.0

Retail Price $249.95

•Easily adjust the Contrast or Brightness of your photo! Your photos don't have to be perfect, just fix it with QPD 2.0!

•You get more design options… Gray scale, Realistic, Sepia Tones!

•You have full control of the number of squares and the number of fabrics!

•You get complete control of the finished dimensions of the quilt. So now you can easily design an art quilt that is the perfect size to fit your wall!

•You can see a preview of the pattern be fore you print it out! The patterns now have large numbers!!!

•The palette has large color swatches! Print it out to match your fabrics!

•You can also import your own fabrics into the preview and see your quilt before you cut even one fabric!!

Video Demos at: HowToSewArt.com

Color Valuations Software 2.0

Finally, Sorting your fabric by Color Value Is Easy Just click the button and your fabrics are sorted! You can print out your fabrics sorted and in full color! Create your own visual fabric collection to take with you when you shop. You can sort the fabrics for one project or even your whole stash!!!

Retail Price $39.95

All software available for XP/2000/Vista / windows 7 & 8, MAC

Windows Requirements
Pentium III 500MHz
512MB Ram (recommended)
20MB free HD Space
32MB VRAM video card
Windows 98/ME/XP/2000/Vista
Windows 7 and 8

Mac Requirements
Recommended Systems:
-Mac Mini (Intel Based Only)
-iMac (Intel Based Only)
-Macbook
-Macbook Air
-Macbook Pro
Complete Specifications:
-1GB Ram (recommended)
-20MB free Harddrive Space
-10.5 (Leopard)
- Snow Leopard

Software Comparison Chart

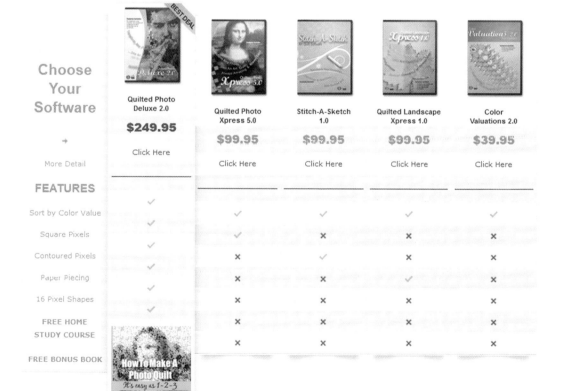

Choose Your Software	Quilted Photo Deluxe 2.0	Quilted Photo Xpress 5.0	Stitch-A-Sketch 1.0	Quilted Landscape Xpress 1.0	Color Valuations 2.0
	$249.95	$99.95	$99.95	$99.95	$39.95
More Detail	Click Here	Click Here	Click Here	Click Here	Click Here
FEATURES					
Sort by Color Value	✓	✓	✓	✓	✓
Square Pixels	✓	✓	✗	✗	✗
Contoured Pixels	✓	✗	✓	✗	✗
Paper Piecing	✓	✗	✗	✓	✗
16 Pixel Shapes	✓	✗	✗	✗	✗
FREE HOME STUDY COURSE	✓	✗	✗	✗	✗
FREE BONUS BOOK	✓	✗	✗	✗	✗

#5525 $14.00
                                    Sugg. Retail

Gerber Daisey Art Quilt Pattern
Raw Edge Applique & Free Motion Quilting

You'll learn how to make this beautiful art quilt using the new **Contoured Pixel Technique**™. Each pattern includes free online video lessons to guide you. Finished quilt size is 27" x 19".

How To SEW ART
...*the easy way!*

FREE
Online Video
Course With
Purchase!
$47.00 value

www.**HowToSewArt**.com

Gerber Daisey Pattern

This beautiful gerber daisey is available as a printed pattern. The pattern includes step by step graphic instructions. $14.00

Value Isolation Postcard
Use this simple tool to sort your fabric by color value! Get one **Free With Every Order!**

Amazing Quilting Film

This package contains 2 yards Iron-off quilting film. This inexpensive film is a priceless aid for easy freemotion quilting. It is visually clear so you can see right through it! Use with 100% cotton fabric only. 40″ wide $7.95

Extra – Wide Fusible Web

This fusible interfacing was carefully tested for use with Quilted Photography projects. It is transparent, lightweight, and has a superior adhesive to firmly hold the fabric swatches in place. The interfacing is 60″ wide and the package contains 2 yards. Imported from France. $15.20

Home Study Video Courses

When you sign up for any of my home study courses, you'll receive the homework, lessons, videos etc via email. You will study your lessons during the week on your own. The lessons will include everything you need to know to successfully complete your home study course. You can work at your own pace… fast or slow, it's up to you.

Simply Amazing Quilted Photography – $47

Learn how to make a pixel quilt with pieced squares. You will learn how to make quilts like the ones in my first book "Simply Amazing Quilted Photography". Each pixel quilt takes only a short time to make and you'll learn the simple sewing technique that will reduce your sewing time by 85%. The quilts look intricate and difficult to make, but it's easy…even if you are just beginning to sew.

More Amazing Quilted Photography – $87

Learn to transform ordinary fabric strips n' pieces into unbelievably beautiful photographic quilts!   In this course you will learn how to make your photo quilts look more painted and less digital. Your friends will be amazed when they realize your quilt is really a photograph! As seen on Friends of Kaye on PBS, and Sewing With Nancy on PBS. One of Tammie's quilts made with this technique was bought by the Shelbourn Museum in 2011. This course is all inclusive and includes fabric!

Magical Contoured Pixel™ – $97

You'll learn how to do this amazing contoured technique. This course will allow you to make quilts that are ART… they catch the attention of all who see them. Even rock stars! My student Jean took the class and her quilt caught the eye of Rod Stewart himself! He even let her go back stage at his concert! Tammie also won the attention of the judges at Quilt National '07 and won the Japan Award!

Doodle Art Quilts – $47

This fun course teaches you how to make amazing quilts using drawings or even paintings. Make quilts from your children's or grandchildren's drawings. These cute quilts will keep them warm and will be a keepsake forever reminding them of when they were small.

Doodlemotion...Free Motion The Easy Way! – $37

In this course, we will explore Free Motion Quilting and how I do it. I call it doodlemotion because it feels like doodling when you get the hang of it.

Fast n' Easy Photo Pillows – $27

This fun course teaches you how to make Pillows and more with almost no work. These projects are made with printable fabric sheets and your printer. We will explore many techniques including photo quilts and traditional quilt styles (all easy). You can use either a laser printer or ink jet printer. The Quilts, wall hangings or pillows you make will look like you spent hours and hours creating but the secret is they only take a short amount of time. Great for gifts!

Making A Profit With Stitched Art – $67

Are you ready to start making a profit with your stitched art? This video course will show you how to turn your art into cash. You'll learn how to find clients, how to promote your work and a strategy for setting your prices. Includes a special video about how to use social media in your marketing.

To Get Full Details Of All Of The Available Home Study Courses Visit Me At:

Notes

Get Stitched Art Quilting Supplies!

Order Form

FREE SHIPPING
on all orders over $100

Shipping Charges

$25.00 and under	$4.95
$25.01 to $49.99	$7.95
$50.00 to $99.99	$10.95
$100 and over	Free

Payment Method

☐ Mastercard
☐ Visa
☐ American Express
☐ Discover
☐ Check
(Payable to: Mosaic Quilt Studio)

FREE
Gift
Included With
Every Order

Description	Unit Price	Qty.	Coupon Code #	Subtotal
Quilted Photo Deluxe 2.0 Software	$249.95			
Stitch-A-Sketch 1.0 Software	$99.95			
Color Valuations Software	$39.95			
Extra Wide Fusible Web	$14.00			
Angelina Fiber Assortment Pack	$8.00			
Amazing Quilting Film	$7.95			
How To Make A Photo Quilt Book	$16.95			
Simply Amazing Book	$29.95			
More Amazing Book	$29.95			
Amazing Chenilled Book	$29.95			
How To Sew Art Book	$29.95			
Gerber Daisey Printed Pattern	$14.00			
Simply Amazng Home Study Course	$47.00			
More Amazng Home Study Course	$87.00			
Doodle Art Quilts Home Study Course	$47.00			
Doodlemotion Home Study Course	$37.00			
Easy Photo Pillows Home Study Course	$27.00			
Profit Stitched Art Home Study Course	$67.00			
Teachers's Certification Course	$447.00			

Total Item Price	
CA residents include 9.2 % sales tax	
Total Shipping	
Total Enclosed	

Shipping Address

Name

Address

City _____ State _____ Zip _____

Phone

Email

Name on Card

Credit Card #

Expires

Signature

Notes

Check List Of Core Concepts, Rules & Success Secrets

Core Concepts

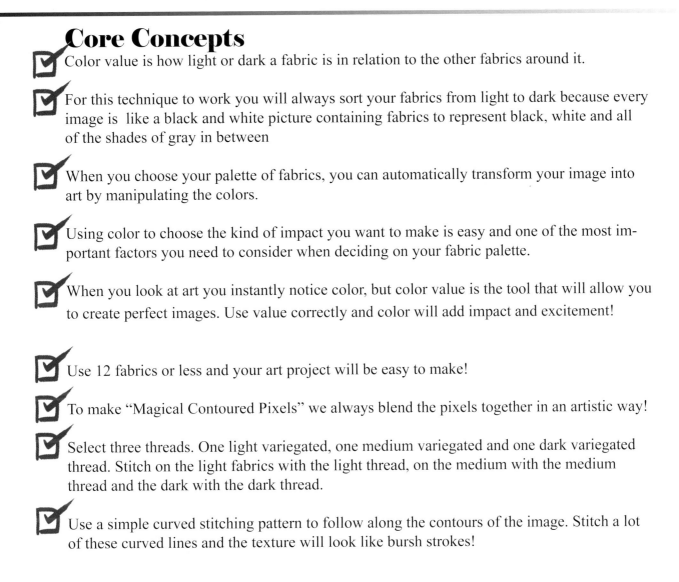

☑ Color value is how light or dark a fabric is in relation to the other fabrics around it.

☑ For this technique to work you will always sort your fabrics from light to dark because every image is like a black and white picture containing fabrics to represent black, white and all of the shades of gray in between

☑ When you choose your palette of fabrics, you can automatically transform your image into art by manipulating the colors.

☑ Using color to choose the kind of impact you want to make is easy and one of the most important factors you need to consider when deciding on your fabric palette.

☑ When you look at art you instantly notice color, but color value is the tool that will allow you to create perfect images. Use value correctly and color will add impact and excitement!

☑ Use 12 fabrics or less and your art project will be easy to make!

☑ To make "Magical Contoured Pixels" we always blend the pixels together in an artistic way!

☑ Select three threads. One light variegated, one medium variegated and one dark variegated thread. Stitch on the light fabrics with the light thread, on the medium with the medium thread and the dark with the dark thread.

☑ Use a simple curved stitching pattern to follow along the contours of the image. Stitch a lot of these curved lines and the texture will look like bursh strokes!

Success Secrets
#1 Pick A Good Subject
#2 Choose Great Fabric
#3 The Magic Contoured Technique
#4 Use Thread Like A Paint Brush!

Rules For Choosing Batiks, Prints & Patterns
Rule #1 Only use fabrics that have a consistent color value. If the fabrics have more than one color, they must be in the same value family.
Rule #2 Try to avoid prints that have a background that is too highly contrasted.
Rule #3 Avoid tie dyed fabrics because the color value can change drastically from one area of the yardage to another.

About The Author

Tammie Bowser

I began sewing at four years old. I made my own clothing in jr. high and high school. I went on to fashion college (The Fashion Institute of Design and Merchandising). I studied fashion design, color theory and pattern making then graduated in 1985. My 18 year fashion career included positions as a fashion designer, production patternmaker and a first patternmaker.

I remember watching "Quilt In A Day" with Eleanor Burns on PBS but never tried to make one until I was at home after my daughter was born (fall of 2000). I began to read books about quilting. I made my first quilt as a gift for my mother in November of 2000. I taught myself how to quilt by reading books, and watching the HGTV series, "Simply Quilts".

After making that first quilt, I wanted to design my own quilts. A few weeks later, I woke up with the beginnings of the ideas you learned in this book.

Look for me on Quilting Arts TV in Season 1500, 1600 and on Sewing With Nancy in 2015.

I am available to make commissioned stitched art for private clients.

I am also available to teach you or your group how to be an artist!

If you are interested, contact me at: **www.TammieBowser.com**

How To Claim Your Free Video Course

At the beginning of this book, I promised to give you a magical experience. To make sure that I deliver on my promise, you need to watch the video lessons that I've prepared for you. You will receive email messages from me with video links, access to my private student website as well as opportunities to ask me your personal questions!

When you come to the website, click on the link labeled "Free Bonuses". Because you purchased this book, you are entitled to this video course for free. For non-students this course is priced at $97. All you have to do is enter your email address then follow the instructions on the screen.

Thank you and I'll see you in the online class!

"If you've looked at Tammie Bowser's amazing art quilts and thought, 'How does she do that?' or 'I could never make something so beautiful!' this book is your answer. Tammie breaks down her creative process and construction techniques into manageable bites, and explains it in simple language, so that anyone can learn it. Beyond the solid information and instructions, this book is an intimate look inside the mind and heart of a unique fiber artist with a great passion for teaching."
Susan Brubaker Knapp
Fiber artist, author, and host of Quilting Arts TV

"Tammie's quilted photos are so slick to make; they come together like magic! Besides being fun to make, It's fun to bask in all the compliments."
Ami Simms
Quilt book author, award winning quilter

"Tammie Bowser's methods give you the tools to make heirloom quality quilts on your first try. She has created a program that breaks down a process that would be unfathomably complicated for a busy quilter and makes it fun and fast to do. The results are nothing short of stunning in every case."
Sue Ann Taylor
Founder of Quilters News Network

"Your favorite photos recreated in fabric... what a fabulous idea! Tammie's easy to follow directions and her color value theories will help you preserve a memory in fabric"...
Kaye Wood
Television show host and author of 28 quilting books